MW01222087

Titles in the series

www.amazingstoriesbooks.com

LATE-BREAKING
AMAZING STORIES™

DANGEROUS DOGS

When pets turn nasty

by Roxanne Willems Snopek

PUBLISHED BY ALTITUDE PUBLISHING LTD.
1500 Railway Avenue, Canmore, Alberta T1W 1P6
www.amazingstoriesbooks.com
1-800-957-6888

Extreme care has been taken to ensure that the information contained
in this book is accurate and up to date at the time of printing. However,
neither the author nor the publisher is responsible for errors, omissions,
loss of income or anything else that may result from the information
contained in this book.

All web site URLs mentioned in this book were correct at the time
of printing. The publisher is not responsible for the content of
external web sites or changes which may have occurred since publication.

In order to make this book as universal as possible, all currency
is shown in U.S. dollars.

Publisher	Stephen Hutchings
Associate Publisher	Kara Turner
Canadian Editor	Deborah Lawson
U.S. Editor	Julian Martin
Charts & Layout	Bryan Pezzi

We acknowledge the financial support of the Government
of Canada through the Book Publishing Industry Development
Program (BPIDP) for our publishing activities.

ALTITUDE GREENTREE PROGRAM
Altitude Publishing will plant twice as many trees as were used
in the manufacturing of this product.

Cataloging in Publication Data

ISBN 1-55265-312-9 (American mass market edition)
ISBN 1-55439-515-1 (Canadian mass market edition)

    1. Dog attacks--Canada. I. Title. II. Series.

SF433.S66 2006a	363.7'8	C2006-901247-4 (U.S.)
SF433.S66 2006	363.7'8	C2006-901248-2 (Cdn)

In Canada, Amazing Stories® is a registered trademark of Altitude Publishing
Canada Ltd. An application for the same trademark is pending in the U.S.

Printed and bound in Canada by Friesens
2 4 6 8 9 7 5 3 1

"It's not one particular breed of dog that is vicious; all dogs have teeth and can use them."

Jeff Armstrong, father of mauling victim Ryan Armstrong

CONTENTS

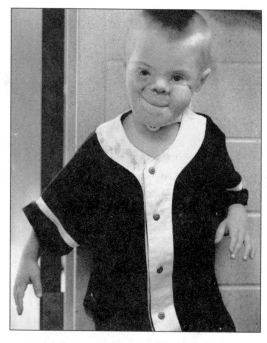

Mycha Lee Herbert, aged two and a half, at
the Children's Medical Center in Dallas. In August
1998, Mycha was attacked by the family dog. After the
attack, his face was reduced to bone from the bottom
of his eyes to his throat. Other vicious dog attacks
are recounted in Chapter 1.

Eight-year-old Annette Rojas at the Santa Rosa
Memorial Hospital, June 24, 2005, in Santa Rosa,
California. Annette and her mother were attacked by
a pit bull that entered their property through an open
gate. For more on Annette's story, turn to page 16.

Robert Noel and Marjorie Knoller in court in San
Francisco, 2001, after their dog fatally mauled Diane
Whipple. Noel was later charged with involuntary manslaughter and Knoller, who was present at the time of
the attack, was charged with second-degree murder
and involuntary manslaughter. For more
on this story, see Chapter 3.

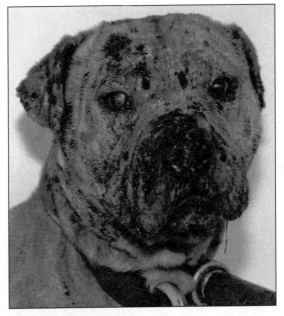

The scarred face of a pit bull that was removed along
with 21 others from a property in New Jersey. The
owner was arrested on charges of mistreating the dogs
with the intent of training the animals for dogfights.
For the story on dogfighting, see Chapter 3.

Cynthia Carstensen is licked by her 11-month-old
pit bull, Herbert, during a protest. Dozens of
demonstrators brought their pit bulls to the offices
of the *Palo Alto Daily News* in Palo Alto, California,
May 18, 2005, to protest the decision to exclude
pit bulls from the paper's "Pet of the Week"
columns due to their violent nature.

Jeff Armstrong, right, sits with his son, Ryan, at their home in Illinois, December 2005. Ryan was seriously injured in a dog attack and his father has become an advocate for stricter laws to crackdown on vicious dogs. For more on dog legislation, see Chapter 6.

CHAPTER 1

"Another Vicious Dog Attack!"

From the *Vancouver Sun*

On December 22, 2002, at about 1:30 a.m., Vancouver, British Columbia, high school student Shenica White was returning to a slumber party with a friend after walking a third girl to her home nearby, when two mastiff/rottweiler-type dogs ran toward them. The dogs, normally confined to a fenced yard, had escaped some time earlier, unbeknownst to their owner. Excited by their unexpected freedom, they responded to the girls' fear by attacking, focusing on White. Neighbors heard screams and rushed out, but before they were able to chase the dogs away White had been savagely mauled. Her scalp was torn away from her skull in places. She'd received deep wounds to her face and arm. She spent two weeks in a hospital and has had eight operations, including several skin grafts, to repair the damage and the surgeons aren't finished with her yet. The owner, who only discovered his dogs' role in the attack when he went to pick them up at the city pound, was devastated. Both dogs were euthanized, with the owner's consent.

From the *San Francisco Chronicle*

Just before noon on June 22, 2005, in Santa Rosa, California, eight-year-old Annette Rojas was playing outside when Smokey, the pit-bull-type dog who was living temporarily with the next-door neighbor, escaped. He ran to Annette's yard and attacked her, clamping his jaws around her face and attempting to drag her away. Annette's mother, Norma Flores, and two nearby men ran to help, beating the dog with a pool cue, a crowbar and eventually prying the dog off the girl with their bare hands, after which he turned on the woman. When Annette and her mother were finally able to get away, they ran inside the house to call police, while the men tried to trap the dog in the garage.

The dog was taken into quarantine by animal control officers and euthanized the following week. Annette Rojas and her mother were taken to a hospital where the mother was treated and released. The daughter, however, suffered more than 50 injuries to her arm and neck, some perilously close to her carotid artery. She also received deep facial lacerations that will leave permanent scars.

These attacks are not the worst. Every year, a handful of dog bites will be so severe that the victims will not survive their injuries. Most of these victims will be either young children or elderly people.

From the *Richmond Times-Dispatch*

On Sunday, April 10, 2005, four-year-old Robert Schafer wandered into the backyard where the family dog, a male rottweiler/German shepherd cross named Chance, was confined. The Schafer family lived in a mobile-home park in rural Virginia. They'd had the dog since before Robert's birth. Laura Schafer, the boy's mother, had just gone inside when she heard the screams. She rushed out and pulled the dog off her son, but it was too late. An autopsy revealed that the boy's neck had been broken. Chance had never before exhibited signs of aggression and had always played well with the boy. No charges were laid but the owners relinquished Chance to animal control authorities. He was later euthanized.

Associated Press reports described, only a month earlier, a similar attack in neighboring Spotsylvania County, Virginia. Dorothy Sullivan, an 82-year-old woman, was walking her dog when three pit-bull-type dogs attacked. Sullivan died of her injuries before reaching hospital; her dog was also killed. A charge of involuntary manslaughter was laid against Deanne Hilda Large, identified as one of the owners of the three pit-bull-type dogs.

From various newspapers, Spring 2005

On March 14, 2005, Kenneth Gamble returned to the Houston, Texas, home he shared with two dogs and with 33-year-old Sandra Sanchez, who had been renting a room from him for about six months. Sanchez was well acquainted with the animals, one rottweiler and one mixed-breed dog.

But when Gamble arrived home that night, he walked in on the grisly sight of Sanchez lying on the blood-soaked ground with his dogs hovering over her lifeless body. Autopsy reports indicated that the woman had received multiple dog bites to her head and torso, resulting in death by blood loss. Without witnesses, no one can conclusively state the circumstances of the incident, but Gamble immediately relinquished both dogs to animal control officials, who destroyed them.

From the *San Francisco Chronicle*

On January 26, 2001, a San Francisco woman named Diane Whipple died after being mauled inside her apartment building by two "bullmastiffs." The neighbor, with whom the dogs lived, was physically unable to restrain the dogs or pull them off once the attack began. The dogs, Bane and Hera, later identified as presa Canarios, attacked with such ferocity that they shredded Whipple's clothing, lacerated her jugular vein and carotid artery, and crushed her larynx. Both dogs were eventually euthanized. The case went on to become one of the most well-known and controversial examples of a dog attack in America.

From the *Detroit Free Press*

On April 3, 2005, in Hamtramck, Michigan, six-year-old Cassidy Jeter and another child went outside to play on a swing set in another yard.

Two pit-bull-type dogs, owned by the Jeters, saw the children, gave chase and quickly began attacking. They focused on Cassidy, ignoring the other child. When Cassidy's mother heard the screams, she grabbed a nearby two-by-four section of lumber and rushed into the melee, trying unsuccessfully to beat the dogs off. Police officers called to the scene also tried to stop the attack, but were finally forced to shoot and kill the dogs on site. Cassidy Jeter was pronounced dead at the scene.

From Canadian Press reports

On March 1, 2003, four-year-old James Waddell, who lived with his father, Ron Waddell, in their home in rural New Brunswick, Canada, opened his door, apparently to go out in search of his father. Waddell had left James upstairs in the house watching television while he went to work in the basement, which was accessible only by going outside and through the backyard. Mike Clark, a family friend who had been living on the property with them for the past several months, went to the basement also to give Waddell a hand. Unbeknownst to Waddell however, Clark had released his three rottweilers from a backyard pen in which they were usually housed.

When little James opened the front door to look for his father, the three dogs outside attacked him and dragged him to the back of the house. When Ron Waddell returned to check on his son, he found instead a trail of blood leading to his badly mauled body. James Waddell, who would have turned five years old the following week, died at the scene. The dogs were seized and later euthanized at the request of their owner.

Each year, hundreds of thousands of potentially violent confrontations occur between dogs and people. Some are relatively minor, little more than a show of bluff and swagger. Other interactions are interrupted before they reach full volume, either because someone correctly recognizes the dog's behavior and withdraws the aggression trigger, or because someone in a position of authority over the dog is able to stop the animal before it goes too far. But the fact is, the Centers for Disease Control and Prevention in Atlanta, Georgia, reports that over four million Americans are treated for dog bites every year. One out of every six bites is serious enough to require medical treatment and 10 to 20 of these will prove fatal. Although Canada has no mandatory reporting of dog-bite injuries, the Canada Safety Council estimates that 460,000 Canadians suffer dog bites each year. Statistically, at least one death due to dog-bite injuries can be expected each year in Canada.

But the worst part of this tragic scenario is that most of these victims—the majority of whom were children—need not have died. The American Humane Association says that dog bites present a risk to children that trump measles, mumps and whooping cough combined. Apparently, North American children need a shot of dog-bite prevention as well.

According to Brian Kilcommons, one of the foremost dog trainers in the United States, aggression is a serious concern among dog owners, even responsible, committed owners. "It's one of the major problems," he says, "and like cancer, it's going to kill your dog." Also like cancer, there's much we can do to prevent such aggression from escalating to the point where the dog commits a capital offense leading to its execution.

However, Kilcommons, a former reporter, cautions people to look for all the facts before making conclusions about dog attacks. "If it bleeds, it leads," he says, "so what we get is partial information." Certainly, my research on the cases listed above turned up numerous inconsistencies and contradictory reports. Most of the questionable details didn't change the bare facts of the incidents but what they showed me was that rarely do we read the entire story. "Statistics tell us that one of the things that's true," says Kilcommons, "is that the dogs that bite are usually the neighbor's dog or the family dog. They're not dogs at large." It's similar to the human parallel of attacks by known assailants being more common than random assaults by complete strangers. Unfortunately, as with human sociopaths, when multiple dogs running at large do attack, the results can be horrific, as in the case of Shenica White and Dorothy Sullivan.

Most of these incidents could not truly be called accidents. Contributing factors accelerated the spiral of events that ultimately led to the tragedies. Consider:

- Smokey, the dog that attacked Annette Rojas, was an eight-month old, unneutered male boarding with the neighbor, a woman in her seventies, while his owner was house hunting. Much of Smokey's care was left to this elderly woman and the owner's 13-year-old daughter, neither of whom were capable of managing a high-maintenance dog. Sexually mature dogs that are intact, that is, unneutered males or unspayed females, bite more often than dogs that have been surgically altered.

- Chance, the dog that killed Robert Shafer, was routinely kept on a chain in a fenced backyard. The use of a chain is a known factor in dog attacks and children between the ages of one and four are at greatest risk of being hurt.

- The dogs that killed Dorothy Sullivan were known and feared by others in the community. Several complaints had been made in the past about these dogs roaming at large.

- Bane and Hera, the dogs that killed Diane Whipple, were both intact adult dogs living with inexperienced dog owners and they had lived in several different homes before that. They'd made numerous threatening advances on others in the community and a veterinarian had previously warned the owners about their dogs' aggressiveness.

- Cassidy Jeter's family was in the process of moving and the dogs had apparently been left unattended for a considerable period of time. Post-mortem reports indicated that not only were the gastro-intestinal tracts of both dogs completely empty, but they'd also recently ingested rat poison. Both dogs, one male and one female, were intact adults.

- Besides the dogs that killed James Waddell, another dog—a female, separated from the others because she was in heat—had been confined to the house. Several sexually mature, intact male dogs near a female in heat present an enormous risk factor for aggression.

No circumstances can excuse the acts of these dogs. Such attacks are capital offenses and the voice of reason is clear: dogs that kill must be killed. But only by examining the circumstances surrounding such tragedies can we understand what led up to them and what steps must be taken to protect ourselves and our children.

CHAPTER 2

Anatomy of Dog Attacks

iven that humans and dogs have lived together in close association for more than 10,000 years, and considering the sheer number of dogs that live as companions, a certain amount of friction is to be expected. However, dog attacks such as these, resulting in serious injury or death, make headlines for a reason: they are the extreme exception. For every newspaper that screams of another death at the jaws of a brutal canine, there are hundreds upon thousands of incidents of dogs exhibiting nothing but ferocious love for their owners and an incredible tolerance for strangers.

NUMBER OF DOGS AS PETS IN THE UNITED STATES AND CANADA

In the United States there are more than 60 million pet dogs (and 70 million cats).
Source: American Veterinary Medical Association

In Canada there are 5.1 million dogs (7.3 million cats). Thirty percent of Canadian families own a dog.
Source: SPCA Canada

But the indisputable fact remains that within all dogs are the genetic instructions to hunt, kill, and scavenge, to work together as a team, and to use any force necessary to protect themselves and their territory. They have all the physical characteristics necessary to do this work effectively.

Humans have successfully manipulated this species to suit our needs but we will never be able to eradicate entirely their potential for violence, nor would we wish to do so. We are grateful for the dog's protective nature when he alerts us to the presence of an intruder. We praise the dog's predatory skills when he dispatches a rat in the backyard. Few sights are more entertaining than two friendly dogs chasing and wrestling with each other, despite the fact that even during such games, they are honing their fighting tactics.

Wolves Under the Skin

When comparing the mitochondrial DNA (mtDNA) of 140 dogs of 67 different breeds with that of 162 wolves of four different subspecies, researchers at the University of California, Los Angeles, discovered recently that dogs are more closely related to wolves than was previously thought. They are close enough, in fact, as to be the same species. The coyote, by comparison, is merely a distant cousin to the wolf.

Looking at a German shepherd or a malamute, it's not hard to see the resemblance. But a Maltese? A dachshund? A poodle? It's still there. Genetically similar does not mean genetically the same; we humans are, after all, genetically similar to chimpanzees. Nevertheless, all dogs, regardless of breed, have the same genetic link to wolves and we would do well to remember that fact. In their book, *Dogs: A New Understanding of Canine Origin, Behavior and Evolution*, Raymond and Lorna Coppinger explain that instead of a simple dogs-evolving-from-wolves scenario, it's more likely that wolves and dogs both descend from a common and now-extinct ancestor.

DOG GENETICS

"Dogs are gray wolves," writes Robert K. Wayne, Ph.D., professor of biology at UCLA. "A limited mtDNA restriction fragment analysis of seven dog breeds and 26 gray wolf populations from different locations around the world has shown that the genotypes of dogs and wolves are either identical or differ by the loss or gain of only one or two restriction sites. The domestic dog is an extremely close relative of the gray wolf, differing from it by at most 0.2 percent of mtDNA sequence. In comparison, the gray wolf differs from its closest wild relative, the coyote, by about 4 percent of mitochondrial DNA sequence."

Robert K. Wayne,
"Molecular Evolution
of the Dog Family"

Regardless of the scientific theory, selective breeding over thousands of years has pinpointed and exaggerated certain physical and behavioral characteristics within this original wolf-like animal. To understand the differences between dog breeds, we must look at how these breeds, and types of dogs, were developed and why.

Breed Origins

Selective breeding has resulted in dogs with very different talents and body types, all stemming from the original use for which they were designed. Kennel clubs organize breeds into groups based on these origins.

Sporting dogs: Also known as gundogs, breeds in this group are bred to work closely with game-bird hunters. These intelligent, responsive dogs include spaniels, pointers, retrievers and setters, and are used in various ways. Some excel at tracking game, others at indicating the location of the target, others at retrieving the bird after it's fallen. Some have multiple uses. Sporting breeds are, for the most part, medium-to-large sized dogs with a great deal of energy.

Herding dogs: This is an old group, comprised of dogs used to control the movement of livestock. It includes collies, corgis and sheepdogs, all dogs known for their keen intelligence and desire to work. Herding dogs use a vestigial remnant of the pack hunting style to gather together a group of prey animals. But instead of barking or biting, sheepdogs "eye" their flock, convincing the animals to move this way or that, with minimal contact. And instead of other pack members, the dogs work with a human herder who directs them with whistles and other signals. Dogs in the herding category are very athletic and active; many of them, like the Hungarian puli or Old English sheepdog, are recognizable by their spectacular coats.

Terriers: This group is made up of mostly small, fearless dogs used to "go to ground" (from the

French terra, meaning earth). They are tenacious rodent hunters and killers, and are known for their alert, bold, curious personalities. Many terrier breeds have tough, wiry coats. Terriers, many of which require firm handling, are known for being energetic, strong-willed and stubborn, with a tendency to scrappiness.

Working dogs: A variety of breeds fall into this category. All are dogs originally developed for a particular task requiring physical strength. These dogs, such as mastiffs, German shepherds, Dobermans, and rottweilers are usually large, strong dogs perfectly suited for jobs requiring brute force, such as pulling heavy loads or driving livestock. Some were primarily bred for use in protecting livestock from predators or guarding property from intruders; often their size alone is sufficient to deter thieves. Breeds in the working group require experienced owners committed to providing the training and exercise required by these dogs. These are the breeds from which many police, military, and protection dogs are chosen.

Hounds: This category, comprised of dogs used to pursue game animals, is broken into two subgroups. Gazehounds or sight-hounds, such as greyhounds, wolfhounds, salukis, and whippets, have keen eyesight and an innate desire and ability to chase moving objects. They are sensitive-natured, streamlined, muscular dogs with little body fat and they can run like the wind. Scent-hounds such as beagles, foxhounds, bloodhounds, and bassett hounds use their prodigious olfactory abilities to track and find prey. These dogs are built for stamina rather than speed. Both scent-hounds and sight-hounds can be frustrating to train, as they were developed to work as part of a larger group of dogs, rather than for humans. All hounds can be single-minded to a fault when on the trail.

Toys: This group includes such dogs as Pekingese, Pomeranians, Maltese, and Chihuahuas, as well as some tiny versions of larger breeds, such as toy poodles. Many of these dogs were originally kept only by the upper class or royalty. Their primary purpose was companionship, but their owners enjoyed another benefit: parasites would leave the human and go to the dog instead! This group contains the smallest breeds, many of which were developed specifically for their ability to bond with humans.

Non-Sporting: This catchall group includes dogs that don't fit well into any other category. Most are dogs that are primarily used as companions, even though they may have originally been bred for a different purpose. Miniature and standard poodles fit into this category, as do chow-chows, Boston terriers, keeshonden, bulldogs, and shih-tzus.

The Right Dog for the Right Person

Many dog experts can predict exactly which owners will have problems controlling their dogs, simply by looking at the kind of dog they've chosen. Buying a dog should never be done on the spur of the moment, emphasizes Kilcommons, co-author with Sarah Wilson of *Paws to Consider: Choosing the Right Dog for You and Your Family.* "You're bringing a predator and carnivore into your home [that is] going to be intimate with the people that mean the most to you," he says. "And purebred dogs were created for specific functions. You need to know what those are."

Many of the breeds frequently mentioned as potentially dangerous dogs belong to the working group. Large and strong, these are usually poor choices for first-time dog owners. These are not "bad" dogs, but they are high-maintenance dogs that may well turn into bad dogs if their abilities and energy are not properly channeled.

In May 2005, New York resident Melanie Coronetz was walking her dogs, one black Labrador-mix and two schipperkes on leash in the city's Central Park, as she had done for the past 10 years; one was a show champion. Schipperkes, a small Belgian breed, weigh around 15 pounds (7 kg) each. "It was just after dark," remembers Coronetz, "and suddenly, out of nowhere, a free-running rottweiler attacked them." Coronetz screamed for help and beat on the dog but nothing stopped him. Within seconds, both the schipperkes were mauled and bleeding. Coronetz gathered their broken bodies and rushed to New York's famed Animal Medical Center, but it was too late. One was dead on arrival and the other succumbed to his injures several hours later. The rottweiler, which never turned on Coronetz, was easily captured by police and taken away. Shelter workers recognized it as a dog they had recently placed in a new home. The dog was put down several days later.

Rottweilers, and other working/guarding breeds require a higher level of commitment and expertise than other breeds. Maintaining a healthy relationship requires daily maintenance by informed owners willing to do whatever is necessary to mold their dog into a well-mannered member of society. Aggressive behavior may be seen in any breed, but public perception makes it even more important that these large-breed dogs be immaculately trained. "Some toy poodles are sweethearts, some are nasty," says Kilcommons. "One of the best dogs I've ever had in my life was a rottweiler. I'm still in love with the breed, but at this point in my life I wouldn't get another one. Every six months or so, they're going to turn around and look at you and say, 'I think I'm going to be the boss now.'"

Many canine behavioral problems stem from a poor "fit" between dog and owner. A border collie, for example, is a poor choice for a sedentary person who prefers indoor activities. Such highly intelligent, active dogs require a great deal of exercise and interaction with their owners, and thrive when given the opportunity to solve problems. They love to participate in dog sports; agility, flyball, and obedience are full

POPULAR DOG SPORTS

Many canine events emphasize the particular skills of certain breeds, while other events are open to any breed.

Classic Events for Purebreds
- Conformation—at these signature kennel club events, purebred dogs are judged against breed standards.
- Obedience—tests the precision and accuracy of a dog's response to commands.

Exciting Games to Play or Watch
- Agility—timed obstacle courses that challenge obedience, fitness, and handler–dog teamwork.
- Flyball—a relay race involving two teams of dogs jumping obstacles to get to a ball.
- Rally—sometimes called Rally-O, this sport is said to be the link between Canine Good Citizen (CGC) and obedience or agility. Dog and handler proceed through a series of exercises and are judged on the performance at each station.
- Musical Freestyle—similar to equine dressage, freestyle has roots in obedience, but requires many more movements from the dog and handler in a routine set to music.
- Canine Disc—clubs and competitions for dogs that enjoy catching a flying disc.

POPULAR DOG SPORTS (CONTINUED)

Events Highlighting Breed-Specific Skills
- Herding—tests and trials allow herding breeds to demonstrate their ability to perform the tasks for which they were developed.
- Tracking—events demonstrate a dog's ability to recognize and follow human scent, a skill that is useful in the service of mankind. Although scent-hounds such as bloodhounds excel, other breeds compete as well.
- Earth Dog—provides an opportunity for terriers, bred to hunt small game above and below ground, to demonstrate their ability.
- Field Trials—different hunting breeds compete against each other, demonstrating their specific skills. Pointers, retrievers and spaniels each have their own classes.
- Lure Coursing—sight-hounds such as greyhounds and whippets chase an artificial lure, in an open field and are judged on overall ability, speed, endurance, agility, and on how well they follow the lure.
- Sledding—teams of sled dogs race against each other. Northern breeds excel but other large-breed dogs also compete.
- Skijoring—races between teams of sled-dogs pulling handlers on cross-country skis.
- Water Rescue—clubs and competitions for Newfoundland dogs to demonstrate their ability to assist people escaping from boating accidents.
- Weight Pulling—like a tractor pull, this game works

POPULAR DOG SPORTS (CONTINUED)

to see which dog can pull the heaviest weight on a non-wheeled sledge. Sled dogs and other strong working breeds love to compete in these events.

Protection Sports
- Schutzhund (from the German word for "protection dog")—this sport involves tracking and obedience as well as tasks similar to those required for dogs in police work.
- Ring—various intense and demanding personal protection sports that were developed in France, Belgium, and the Netherlands to test potential breeding stock for working ability.

New Sports
- Coonhound Events—Newly introduced by the AKC, these competitive sports involve bench shows, field trials, night hunts and water races to demonstrate the beauty and natural abilities of purebred coonhounds.
- Big Air/Diving Dog—this sport involves a dog racing down a dock and leaping into the water for a thrown object. The longest leap wins.

of border collies. Ignoring this need for stimulation and work can result in dogs creating their own entertainment, perhaps dismantling the furniture or removing the wallpaper. This type of behavior is unwelcome in even the most pet-friendly home, but it can hardly be blamed on the dog. A relatively inactive owner requires a dog with lower exercise needs. An adult rescue greyhound on the other hand, who has been retired from the track and placed in a home as a pet, would be perfect for an owner interested in a dog sport such as lure coursing, but would probably frustrate someone determined to succeed in other dog sports.

Sara Nugent is President of the Staffordshire Terrier Club of America and a former breeder of champion American Staffordshire terriers (also known as AmStaffs) in Houston, Texas. As much as she loves her breed, she knows that not all homes are suitable for them. "I don't tell people that everyone should have one," she says. "They're strong dogs, bright dogs, but if you just put them out in the backyard they'll get into trouble."

Consider also the question of gender. Statistics gathered by the Centers for Disease Control show that of 28 human deaths caused by individual dog attacks, male dogs were responsible for all but two of the deaths. Twenty-one of these males were not neutered; the status of the remaining five was unknown. "What does this tell us?" says Kilcommons. "If you're a first-time dog owner, get a female! Or neuter your male dog."

When inexperienced owners choose a powerful breed because it looks "tough" or will confer status on them, it can have dire consequences. Even the most easy-going breeds have a "terrible twos" stage, that starts around four to six months of age, in which they test their boundaries. A dog with dominant tendencies will attempt to gain control over its owners during this time and will be obnoxious beyond belief. Animal shelters are overflowing with large-breed dogs less than one year old, relinquished by people unprepared for the challenges of raising a dog they should never have gotten in the first place. The rottweiler and mixed-breed dog thought to be responsible for the death of Sandra Sanchez were both young animals, referred to as "puppies" in one news report. "Most of the dogs in the shelter system are juvenile delinquents," Kilcommons says bluntly. "They're good dogs that have been ignored, isolated and punished, but never trained."

Sometimes in an attempt to do the right thing, people will keep a dog that is beyond their handling abilities, but consign it to the basement, the backyard, or the end of a chain. This simply compounds the original mistake. A dog living in such an environment will never receive sufficient socialization, training, or bonding to be a good companion. Worse yet, such conditions will make a dog with aggressive tendencies even more likely to become a statistic. "That's gulag for a dog," says Kilcommons. "They go insane. The most humane thing you can do with a dog that's dangerous is to euthanise him. It's just a matter of time before there's a child bitten and then the dog's euthanized anyway."

Many resources are available to help prospective dog owners evaluate their own lifestyle and decide what qualities to look for in a dog. "I think it's extremely important to research specific breeds," says Kim Moeller of the San Francisco SPCA shelter, who evaluates the dogs there and helps place them in appropriate homes. "A lot of times, people who work 10 hours a day want a dog like a Labrador retriever. It's probably not an appropriate dog for them because of its energy level." Another fallacy, she adds, is that many people assume small dogs are easier for city-dwellers to care for. But that's not always the case. "A lot of times we find that larger dogs actually adjust to apartment living better than some small dogs," she says. Learning about the different breed characteristics, as well as the specifics about the lines of dogs within the cho-

POPULAR PUREBREEDS

According to 2005 statistics from the American Kennel Club (AKC), the most popular dog of all would be the lowly mutt. However, here are some interesting figures about America's nearly one million purebred dogs.

North America's most popular purebred dogs:
1. Labrador retrievers—almost 138,000 Labs were registered in 2005, more than twice as many as any other breed
2. Golden retrievers—just over 48,000 registered in 2005
3. Yorkshire terriers—rose from fifth place in 2004 to third with more than 47,000 dogs registered in 2005
4. German shepherds—dropped from third place in 2004 with about 45,000 registrations in 2005
5. Beagles—almost 43,000 registrations in 2005
6. Dachshunds—almost 39,000
7. Boxers—just over 37,000
8. Poodles—almost 32,000
9. Shih-tzus—just over 28,000
10. Miniature schnauzers—with just over 24,000 registrations, they displaced Chihuahuas for the final spot in 2005's top 10

The Canadian Kennel Club, which registered almost 72,000 dogs in 2005, reflects a similar love for retrievers: Labrador retrievers took top spot, with golden retrievers in second place. German shepherd dogs, poodles, Shetland sheepdogs, Yorkshire terriers, miniature schnauzers, boxers, beagles, and shih-tzus took the remaining top 10 spots.

sen breed, is a good start to making the right choice.

Once aspiring dog owners have established the parameters of care and attention they'll be able to provide, they can begin looking at breeds that are appropriate. Even if all they do is eliminate the breeds that definitely do *not* fit them, it's an exercise well worth doing. Animal behavior specialists and dog trainers are well acquainted with the characteristics of various breeds; veterinarians also see many representatives of different breeds and most have a good feel for the health problems to which various breeds may be susceptible. Many of these experts will also be able to recommend reputable local breeders.

Where to Look

Potential dog owners should definitely not purchase a puppy from either a pet store or a so-called "backyard" breeder. Casual breeders seldom have the knowledge necessary to produce healthy dogs. And pet stores, which are in the business of making money, may have little regard for the well being of their livestock. Many obtain their supply of animals from puppy mills, where adult female dogs are bred repeatedly in order to get as many puppies in as short a time as possible, with no regard for the pup's soundness of either mind or body. Ultimately, with the vast numbers of homeless dogs already in existence, the only real justification for producing puppies is to try and improve the genetics of a breed.

Careful research before bringing that puppy home does not eliminate the possibility of getting a dog with health or behavioral problems, but it improves the odds.

Many excellent family pets have made their way into permanent homes via local shelters or rescue agencies. When shelters do extensive temperament testing on potential adoptees and interview prospective owners to identify the type of dog suitable for them, the chances of a successful outcome shoot up.

HOW TO SPOT AN ETHICAL BREEDER

Good breeders:

- Care more about their dogs than they do about the money they'll make selling the puppies
- Are involved in promoting their breed, either through dog shows, dog sports, or other activities
- Have waiting lists, because they only produce one or two litters each year and their puppies are "spoken for" before birth
- Ensure the genetic soundness of their breeding stock by doing whatever tests are necessary to "breed out" weaknesses inherent in their breed
- Provide evidence, in the form of certification, that the parents are as free as possible of such defects
- Screen their buyers, weeding out those who will not provide good homes
- Insist buyers sign a contract agreeing to have their puppies spayed and neutered, since only dogs sold as potential show and breeding stock should be allowed to remain intact
- Socialize their puppies from birth with regular, gentle handling in a household environment
- Allow potential buyers into their home to see the parents and the environment in which their puppies are born.

Ask for references. Your veterinarian might be able to recommend reputable breeders in your area. So might local grooms and dog trainers. Just as important, they'll be able to tell you which breeders to avoid.

Unfortunately, temperament testing is largely an informal affair. The San Francisco SPCA does what Kim Moeller calls "match-making."

"We tell people, 'This is a particular dog we could offer you.' Maybe we give them three or four choices, based on their lifestyle," she says. "It's not like someone can come in and say, 'I want this particular dog.'" But with its enviable resources and staffing, the San Francisco shelter is, unfortunately, the exception.

"Rescue dogs are a mixed bag," says Dr. Stanley Coren, author of *The Intelligence of Dogs*. "Some are wonderful. Some are potentially loaded guns. You don't know. A lot of shelters, especially the no-kill shelters, either don't keep records or lie about whether dogs have been involved in a biting incident. I'd avoid any breed that could be used in fighting or guarding, because a lot of the dogs [that] come into shelters have been rescued from places like marijuana grow-ops. That dog might need a home, but that dog also might snap at anything that comes near."

Coren agrees that shelters should definitely be using temperament testing. "They're certainly reliable enough to pick out the 'big bads', if not the 'petite mals.'" He also suggests a "test drive" period after which the dog could be brought back if it doesn't fit the new home.

"I raise money for SPCAs and humane societies and I think they're doing a wonderful job," Coren hastens to add. "But their mandate is to get the dog a home and sometimes they don't have enough time, or enough knowledge. Plus, there just aren't enough professionals doing this kind of work."

Kim Moeller says, "With some dogs that are adopted from rescues or shelters, owners don't get a full diagnostic of what this animal is like. They're bringing home baggage the shelter wasn't aware of, and that they themselves weren't aware of, and some of this is genetic." If a dog has a high prey drive, for instance, and attacks other dogs off leash, she advises that the dog must be taught impulse-control, given lots of exercise, socialized to a wide variety of stimulating situations, and develop a strong bond with the owner. "But some things you can't 'train out', so to speak," adds Moeller. "Like prey drive. This is where educating the owner becomes our main focus. We tell them, 'This dog can't go to dog parks, it can't be off leash, and it should be muzzled when outside. If you're going to live with this dog, this is what to expect: a lifetime of this. Are you willing to manage it?'"

In addition to being an author, Brian Kilcommons is the Director of Training, Animal Care and Control for the City of New York. "The quandary with pit bulls is, we have a kennel full of them here in

WHAT IS PREY DRIVE?

This term has fallen out of favor with scientists and trainers in recent years, but it simply refers to the instinct to chase moving objects. A prey-driven dog focuses intently on its target, and this might be expressed differently in different breeds. Border collies "eye" their sheep, which is actually a form of stalking. Hunting and fighting breeds grab and bring down their prey, while terriers catch, shake, and kill small rodents. A "ball crazy" poodle might also be expressing high prey drive.

New York City, and about half of them should be adopted out. But about a third of them should be euthanized. I've had absolute sweethearts. I've had nightmares. This is where temperament testing and evaluation comes in."

Testing a Dog's Temperament

There are a variety of ways a dog's personality can be assessed before it goes to a new home. Temperament testing involves evaluating a dog's reactions to a number of specific situations so that, theoretically, his behavior in similar situations can be predicted. Carl Herkstroeter is President of the American Temperament Test Society (ATTS), a national non-profit association that promotes uniform evaluation of canine behavior. Established in 1977, the ATTS conducts seminars, trains and registers temperament evaluators, and awards certificates to dogs 18 months of age and older that pass the requirements of the test.

Herkstroeter reports that most shelters and

humane societies do not use their standardized test. "There are probably a number of reasons," he explains. "Our test is very labor intensive. It takes a minimum of 10 people to conduct a test: six station workers, three evaluators, and one test secretary."

The shelter environment, he adds, is a poor situation in which to assess a dog's personality. The dog may have been under severe stress prior to arrival. He may have been injured or starved and is almost certainly frightened. "We may not see the true picture," says Herkstroeter, "because it takes time, sometimes a long time, to undo these behaviors."

The test, which takes about 12 minutes to complete, assesses the dog's reaction to strangers, both neutral and friendly, to sudden, sharp noises such as gunshot, to unusual visual stimuli such as an umbrella snapping open nearby, and to unfamiliar tactile stimuli. The dog is then subjected to controlled provocation in the form of a suspicious-looking stranger behaving in a threatening manner 38 feet (11.5 m) away. The dog is on a 6-foot (1.8 m) leash for the entire test and the stranger never gets to within 10 feet (3 m) of the dog. The handler is not allowed to talk to the dog, or give commands or corrections.

"As the dog/handler team progresses through the test," says Herkstroeter, "the stress on the dog builds. We measure the responses to the various subtests. Each test is more stressful than the previous one and it's very difficult for dogs to hide their true feelings."

At the end, the handler is given a critique of the dog's performance and, if successful, will receive a certificate. If the dog shows unprovoked aggression, panic without recovery, or a strong unwillingness to proceed, he automatically fails. All dogs tested, listed according to breed, become part of their database. But prospective dog owners looking at the scores of various breeds should be sure they understand how to interpret those scores. "Just because a certain percentage of dogs in a certain breed fail, this does not necessarily indicate aggression," cautions Herkstroeter. "Dogs fail for other reasons, such as strong avoidance. If you look at our statistics just from a perspective of aggression or non-aggression, they can be very misleading."

Timidity can be a risk factor for fear biting, a defensive, rather than offensive type of aggression; however, training and socialization can work wonders for such dogs. Ninety-five percent of dogs that fail do so not because of aggression, but because of a lack of confidence. They either avoid confrontation with the weirdly dressed stranger or they refuse to walk on the unfamiliar surface. The rest fail because they take longer than 30-45 seconds to recover from the shock of gunshot or the umbrella opening. "I've tested over 8,000 dogs," adds Herkstroeter. "I've had a half-dozen or less fail at the 'friendly stranger' stage. Three or four of these avoided the friendly stranger and two or three showed aggression."

Brian Kilcommons and Sarah Wilson, in

their book *Child-Proofing Your Dog,* suggest several simple ways to evaluate temperament when choosing a puppy. A puppy should calmly allow you to cradle it upside down in your arms like a baby, without panicking. If you pinch him gently between his toes, he should pull away, but immediately relax and "forgive" you. He should recover quickly from a startling sound, such as keys being dropped near him. He should seem interested in being around people. When choosing an adult dog, especially from a shelter, they suggest looking for a dog that comes to the front of the kennel right away, indicating a desire to be with people, but is able to control his excitement. They emphasize the importance of observing how the dog behaves around the people with whom he's already acquainted, such as the shelter staff.

The Rise and Fall of Vicious Dogs

When Diane Whipple was killed in San Francisco in January 2001, widespread media coverage had the unexpected result of shining a spotlight onto a rare, little-known breed. Bane and Hera, the dogs responsible for her death, were presa Canarios, a mastiff-type fighting breed from the Canary Islands. Article after article appeared in newspapers around the world, describing the dogs and their behavior. In the aftermath of the attack and the subsequent courtroom drama, presa Canario breeders were inundated with phone calls from people wanting dogs with a reputation for being aggressive and potentially dangerous. This previously obscure breed hit the popularity charts with a vengeance, driven there largely by unscrupulous owners hoping to gain notoriety by association through their ownership of a "deadly" dog.

At various times historically, other dog breeds have been considered "dangerous." German shepherds and Dobermans have long been favored by the military and police and are often used as security dogs as well. Rottweilers, especially since their portrayal in the movie *The*

Omen, still strike fear into the hearts of many. (Incidentally, the breed's popularity skyrocketed after the film's release.) Chow-chows, with their one-owner loyalty and aloofness to strangers, also have a "use caution" reputation. But other breeds involved in serious or fatal attacks on humans include mastiffs, Great Danes, boxers, and even Labrador retrievers.

"The image aspect has always been around," says Coren. "In New York City, there's an operation called Rent-a-Rottie. Men can pay to rent this big dog with a big chain collar, and they can march around with it for the weekend, looking macho and 'bad' and everyone thinks they have a big, tough dog at home."

"One really cannot compare one breed to another without also taking into account the purpose of the breeds compared. Some breeds have a tendency towards more aggression than others because of what they were bred for, 'way back when," explains Herkstroeter. "However, with training and socialization, these dogs should not be considered dangerous. When dogs are dangerous, either they've been bred to be somewhat aggressive, trained for it, or neglected by their owners."

When it comes to temperament testing, it's the conscientious owners who've worked with their dogs that take part. Herkstroeter doesn't see the people who deliberately encourage unstable, aggressive behavior in their dogs. In other words, those that need the most help with their dogs are the least likely to access it.

"I maintain that when dogs become aggressive, it may not necessarily be the breed," says Herkstroeter, "but the breeder, the owner, and the trainer that are responsible."

Aggression Triggers

Incidents of aggression, if looked at from the dog's point of view, usually have a specific cause. Animal behaviorists, trainers, veterinarians, and psychologists have identified a number of specific types of aggression.

- **Territorial aggression:** This behavior involves a dog protecting property he considers to be his. This might be a yard, a house, a room, or a bed. Dogs often mark the perimeters of "their" outdoor territory with urine to warn off other dogs. In the United States between 1965 and 2001, 11 cases were recorded of children being attacked and killed after somehow getting into kennels or pens housing dogs.

- **Possessive aggression:** Similar to territorial aggression, possessive aggression is more object-specific. Dogs that growl when approached while eating or chewing on a toy are exhibiting possessive aggression. Many, many attacks involve a person coming between a dog and its food. Under certain circumstances, even feeding time can stimulate sufficient excitement to trigger aggression in some dogs. Most new owners are instructed to teach their puppies that they must relinquish anything at anytime, if the owner demands it. But most parents also wisely teach their children never to bother the dog when eating, to prevent this aggression from occurring.

• **Fearful aggression:** This is the "fight" in the "fight-or-flight" response, and is usually seen in poorly socialized or naturally unconfident dogs overwhelmed by an unfamiliar situation. A trip to the animal hospital can trigger fear biting in such a dog. Fuelled by fearful aggression, a dog may behave as if it were literally fighting for its life. Dogs in the throes of such terror are usually completely out of control, snarling and screaming, biting blindly, and urinating and defecating in their frenzied attempts to defend themselves.

• **Predatory aggression:** Dogs instinctively want to chase things that move. In a pack situation, such behavior is effective in bringing down prey. In a home situation, it's relatively uncommon to see actual attacks that stem from this instinct, but it's what stimulates dogs to chase cars, cats, bicycles or running children. Whether or not they cause damage, they certainly appear to have the intent of intimidation, if not of biting. The dogs that killed Dorothy Sullivan were almost certainly acting out of predatory aggression.

• **Intra-sexual aggression:** In the pack hierarchy, there is one male leader and one female leader; all others fit into subordinate roles. Male dogs that pick fights with other males or females that insist on dominating other females are exhibiting intra-sexual aggression. Most multiple-dog owners will have observed that dogs get along together better with a dog of the opposite sex. Intact animals will always display more intra-sexual aggression than those that are spayed and neutered. James Waddell died, at least in part, because he inadvertently got in between a group of intact dogs, one of which was in heat.

• **Parental aggression:** This results from the instinct to guard and protect offspring and is the most well-known reason for caution. Even the most docile female dog will be watchful when strangers approach her puppies and even non-dog people know to respect this instinct. However, while many family dogs are perfectly trustworthy with human infants and children, it should never be assumed the dog would feel the same protectiveness toward them as she would toward her own puppies.

• **Dominance aggression:** This is perhaps the most dangerous type of aggressive behavior, because it stems directly from the desire to be "top dog." A dog exhibiting dominance aggression will stand tall and still, make direct eye contact and probably growl. Dogs at risk of dominance aggression constantly challenge the demands made upon them by their humans, for example, growling if asked to get off the couch, or deliberately ignoring or disobeying commands. The human-dog relationship only functions properly when the human is in charge, but it is in the nature of dogs to always be on the lookout for opportunities to move up in status. Two very dominant dogs with no respect for human authority killed Diane Whipple. Some dogs are naturally more dominant than others and size, while not always an indicator, plays a role. Large working-breed dogs often have dominant personalities; this is part of what makes them effective guard and police dogs. But smaller dogs, such as many terrier breeds, can also be very strong-willed.

"An aggressive individual has a low threshold of aggression," says Coren. "It might be lower for dogs or cats or other things. That threshold will also be lower for people—much lower than you find in well bred dogs."

"You have to differentiate between a dog that grabs you but doesn't do damage, and the dog that grabs and bites down," says Kilcommons. "But the common theme is that teeth do not belong on human flesh, period."

In general, animal behavior experts identify several levels of aggression based on intent and resulting injury. These are classified on the following scale.

- **Level 1:** The dog does not touch the skin. This is simply "air-biting" or snapping and it indicates a dog with excellent bite inhibition. The intent is to give clear warning. Adult dogs often do this, appropriately, when reprimanding rude puppies. Such snapping at a human, however, is inappropriate and a firm indication to begin intervention. Assessment by a qualified behaviorist can help identify the triggers and work to prevent the aggression from escalating.

- **Level 2:** The bite makes contact with the skin without breaking it. Although these can still result in painful bruising, no bleeding or abrasions result. A dog that does this is exhibiting extreme control and is still, primarily, giving a warning.

- **Level 3:** A bite at this level might range from a minor abrasion, to between one and four puncture wounds of less than the depth of the dog's canine or eyetooth, with or without skin tearing. Obviously, a large-breed dog will be able to inflict a deeper bite than a smaller toothed dog. Most Level 3 bites do not require medical attention, but they are still a clear indication of a troubled dog. Few trainers are willing to work with a Level 3 biter. Owners are often advised to have such a dog euthanized.

• **Level 4:** One to four puncture wounds of greater depth than the length of the dog's canine tooth. These bites have pressure behind them, usually cause bruising and may or may not cause skin tearing. Most Level 4 bites will require medical attention. Although the dog definitely intends harm at this point, depending on size, he may also be controlling the full extent of damage possible. In many areas, such a dog will be deemed "dangerous" and can be confiscated by animal control or have severe restrictions put on his movement.

• **Level 5:** Multiple Level 4 bites. This dog is out of control and is making no attempt to harness his biting ability. Chances of rehabilitating such a dog are negligible.

- **Level 6:** The dog has killed. There is no question that this dog *must* be euthanized.

Deadly behavior doesn't happen overnight, according to Kilcommons. "It takes about six months to a year for a dog to build up enough confidence for this behavior, but people do not see the progression." Dogs are constantly watching for changes within the leadership of their "pack." Every time a dog behaves rudely without direction, growls at a person, refuses to give up a toy, or ignores a command, his own status relative to the human increases. He has in effect, "won" several small battles, without the owner even being aware of it. Each such confrontation increases the dog's sense of power, until he believes it is his right to control the relationship.

Without intervention, these situations too often spiral into tragedy.

CHAPTER 3

Dogs and Blood Sports

Diane Whipple's death quickly made news across California and the nation. The "San Francisco Dog Mauling," as it was quickly dubbed, was a deeply disturbing incident. The victim was neither a child, nor an elderly person, but instead, a 33-year-old athletic woman.

The dogs had been obtained by Pelican Bay State Prison inmate and Aryan Brotherhood member Paul Schneider, as breeding stock for a kennel he hoped to establish outside prison, called Dog O' War. Schneider chose his breed carefully; also known as Canary dogs, presa Canarios are big-boned, heavily muscled dogs, weighing around 100 pounds (45 kg), with strong-willed temperaments to match. Bane, the male, weighed about 125 pounds (57 kg). The breed was developed in the 1800s for a very specific purpose: dogfighting.

Schneider insisted

THE PERRO DE PRESA CANARIO BREED

Also known as the Canary dog, or simply presa Canario, this is a powerfully built, square-headed, mastiff-type dog originating in the Canary Islands. Not recognized by either the Canadian Kennel Club or the American Kennel Club, this rare breed is the result of crossing the rare bandino majero with British mastiffs for the express purpose of dogfighting. When the Canary Islands banned dogfighting in the 1940s, the breed almost disappeared. Breed standards describe these dogs as weighing between 85–125 pounds (39–57 kg) and standing 21.5–26.5 inches (55–67 cm) high at the shoulder. Their temperament is said to be quiet, loyal, and eager-to-please, but they are suspicious of strangers and aggressive to other dogs.

that caretakers encourage the aggressive tendencies of his dogs; when a previous caretaker proved unsatisfactory, Schneider instructed that a female named Hera, and later a male called Bane, be turned over to husband-wife team Robert Noel and Marjorie Knoller. Noel and Knoller, incidentally, were Schneider's lawyers. It was a decision that would prove fatal for Diane Whipple.

On the afternoon of her death, as Whipple stood at her door, juggling keys and groceries, Knoller was entering her own apartment down the hall, with Bane on leash at her side. Hera met Knoller at the open door, saw Whipple in the hallway and started growling. This aroused Bane, who dragged Knoller down the hallway and proceeded to attack Whipple. Hera followed his lead. Each of Whipple's defensive movements triggered more aggression, with most of the bites focused on her head and neck.

The attack finally stopped when Whipple lay motionless on the floor in the hallway. Most of her clothing had been ripped off and she was covered in blood. She'd received a total of 77 bite wounds.

A terrified neighbor who heard the snarls and screams called 911. Within minutes, Whipple was rushed to a hospital. For the next five hours, trauma specialists tried to save her, but the worst of the bites had punctured her jugular vein and carotid artery, crushed her larynx, and nearly severed her vertebrae. Ultimately Diane Whipple died of massive blood loss and asphyxiation.

While Bane was destroyed shortly after the event, Hera underwent behavioral testing to determine her own level of aggression and participation in the attack. Astonishingly, the results were inconclusive, even though bits of clothing had been found in Hera's stool. The following January, she was also destroyed.

This tragic death received extensive publicity, both for the gruesome nature of the event and for its groundbreaking consequences.

Marjorie Knoller and Robert Noel were both convicted of involuntary manslaughter and failing to control a mischievous dog. But the most significant result was that Knoller was also pronounced guilty of second-degree murder, due to the actions of her dog, and was sentenced to a prison term of 15-years-to-life. Although this conviction was later overturned, it sent a clear message that reckless dog owners would be held accountable for their dogs' actions. Ultimately, Knoller and Noel were both sentenced to four years in prison. They each served about half their time in prison. Noel was released in 2003 to serve a two-year parole. Knoller was released in 2004 to serve a three-year parole.

This tragic case takes us to another chapter in the history of domestic dogs—their use, not just as assistants to the hunter, but as hunters and killers in their own right.

Gladiators

Canines have long served side-by-side with soldiers in combat. Ancient Egyptian writings dating as far back as 4000 BC depict savage dogs being used as warriors. Huge mastiff battle dogs wearing spiked collars can be seen in bas-relief on Assyrian temple walls. A wooden block print from 86 BC shows a mastiff war dog accompanying a Celtic soldier in Gaul.

As civilization evolved, violence as a form of entertainment rose in popularity. The fighting skills of dogs on the battlefield led to their being pitted in staged battles against a variety of opponents. From the Roman arenas, to the smoke-filled back rooms of English pubs, dogs were put to use for their ability to bite and hold, to shake and crush.

Today, many breeds trace their ancestry to dogs bred for such activity. Most are descended in at least some part from the bulldog of centuries ago, and share several physical traits that allowed them to survive and excel at their bloody skill. A dog of "bully breed" ancestry usually has, to some extent, an undershot jaw, a wide, flat head and a compact, muscular body. This physical makeup gives him the ability to grab his prey with his teeth, hang on and still be able to breathe while the victim fights to get free.

"You must understand that certain dogs were bred for blood sports," says Stanley Coren, whose book, *The Pawprints of History,* describes the role of dogs in human history. "These so-called bear baiting and bull-baiting dogs were put in a pit or arena and had to fight. That's how the bulldog was developed."

Bears were usually chained while bulls were tied or otherwise restrained. Then one or more dogs were let loose to attack them. Both the winners and the losers suffered horribly in these matches, and many an onlooker left the event spattered with blood. Their physical attributes kept these dogs alive while others were slaughtered, but they also possessed a significant, unique temperament characteristic, referred to as "gameness." The value of dogs used for bull- and bear-baiting was in their determination to continue fighting, to the death if necessary. Aficionados revered a dog that refused to give up, despite mortal wounds. Legends arose of dogs whose jaws had to be pried open, even after death, to release them from their prey.

In 1835 British Parliament supported a request from the newly founded Society for the Prevention of Cruelty to Animals to make sports such as bull- and bear-baiting illegal. Frustrated enthusiasts looked for another way to slake their blood lust, and began to pit one dog against another. "Dogfights were very popular," says Coren. "They were cheaper, you could use a smaller venue, and you didn't need to buy [bait]. Henry VIII had his own pit built, and Queen Elizabeth I had her own line of fighting mastiffs."

But pitting dogs against each other, instead of against bulls and bears, changed the type of dog that excelled. Dogs with agility and speed, in addition to bulk, survived better than dogs with only size and muscle power on their side. "In order to get a more agile dog," says Coren, "they bred a number of little bull-and-terrier crosses." The dogs that resulted were smaller and faster, with tremendous gameness. From these dogs came what most people recognize today as "pit bulls."

The Pit Bull "Problem"

No other breed has a history so fraught with politics, prejudice and semantic difficulties. For the purposes of this book, the term "pit-bull-type dog" will be used when the breed is not known but the dog exhibits the physical characteristics typical of either the American pit bull terrier (APBT) or the American Staffordshire terrier.

When settlers brought these bull-and-terrier-type dogs from England and Ireland to the United States in the early 1800s, the American Kennel Club, disgusted by the lower-class crudeness they felt such dogs represented, refused to recognize them. Frustrated by the elitism that kept their dogs from joining the dog fancy, breeders formed the rival United Kennel

Club for the express purpose of recognizing the American pit bull terrier (APBT). Although the UKC now recognizes more than 300 breeds of dogs, the APBT was the first.

The American Kennel Club, however, insisted that the APBT was inextricably linked to images of blood and gore, and refused to budge. It fell to movies and television to change the minds of the American public, which began demanding dogs like "Petey" of *Our Gang* and *Little Rascals* fame, or "the one on the poster" used to promote World War I patriotic spirit. These people had discovered an important, often overlooked attribute of the APBT and its relatives: these reputed fighting dogs were as loving with their owners as they were ruthless with their canine opponents.

This was a deliberately built-in characteristic, vital in even the most successful of dog-killers, according to Sara Nugent. "You had a judge and two handlers in the pit with the dogs," she says, explaining how dogfights traditionally worked. "They'd fight in rounds. After each round, the handlers would separate the dogs, take them to their corners, and sponge them off. Then they'd put them back." A dog that couldn't be safely handled before, during, and after a fight was obviously a huge danger to its owner. It was essential that these dogs allow their owners to tend to their wounds without the owners having to fear being attacked themselves. So, although dog-aggression remains in their genetic makeup, APBTs earned a well-deserved reputation for being wonderful family companions—energetic, affectionate, and trustworthy.

The AKC finally buckled to the growing demand, agreeing to allow dogs registered with the UKC as American pit bull terriers into their ranks, under one condition. They must be renamed American Staffordshire terriers, often referred to today as AmStaffs.

Many people today feel that the American pit bull terrier and the American Staffordshire terrier are more or less the same dog, while others argue vehemently for their distinction. Both are muscular, broad-headed, short-coated dogs of any color, weighing about 40 to 50 pounds (18–23 kg), with cropped or uncropped ears. Some describe the only difference as being that the slightly smaller AmStaffs are the "show" pit bulls while the APBTs are produced, at least in the United States, by those who want to use them for other purposes. Slight distinctions exist in such things as allowable nose color, as defined by the breed standard, but few people outside the show ring care about such details.

"The American Staffordshire terrier is identical to the American pit bull terrier," says Coren. "It *is* the pit bull."

Obviously, politics, language, and the volatile egos of dog fanciers have made this most confusing for the general public. Ultimately, the salient point is that the term "pit bull" has no official meaning. When the phrase is used, the dog in question could be any one of a number of dogs. American pit bull terriers, American

Staffordshire terriers, bull terriers, Staffordshire bull terriers and even American bulldogs have all been lumped into the "pit bull" category. Some people think any dog with a muscular body, broad head, and short coat is a "pit bull." Others associate the term with cropped ears or brindle coloration. Boxers, mastiffs, rottweilers, bull-mastiffs, and crosses of any of these have all been confused by someone, at some point or another, of being "pit bulls."

Underworld Dog Abuse

Sara Nugent says the explosion in popularity of these breeds and crossbreeds only began about two decades ago. When she got her first AmStaff in 1966 there were hardly any of them around. She recalls scanning the paper for pit bull puppy ads, hoping to meet other fans of the breed; she'd see maybe one each month. But that changed in 1973, when the American Dog Owners Association, a group of well-meaning dog lovers, decided to call attention to the cru-

elty of dogfighting, which was still only a misdemeanor in many states. They carried out sting
operations and took photographs, in hopes of
stimulating public outrage sufficient to raise it
to felony status in every state.

The profile of pit-bull-type dogs rose sharp-
ly, but not the way the ADOA had intended. "The
media fell on it like flies," Nugent remembers.
"There was a big dogfight raid in Chicago, and
one breeder, a very flamboyant person, went to
jail." Enjoying his moment in the limelight, this
breeder played up to reporters, tantalizing them
with bizarre stories and stunts, the perfect fod-
der for sensational journalism. "So these dogs
went from being a small secret breed to being a
media monster," says Nugent. "Every idiot who
wanted a bad dog went out and got one."

But, she says, people who wanted a fierce
dog discovered that while these dogs were aggressive to other dogs, they weren't mean to
people. "In the heat of battle, if a dog bit the
handler it was put down," she says. "AmStaffs

are no longer game—they're not bred for that and I can tell you they're pretty awful watch-dogs!" But then these people began introducing large mastiff-type guardian breeds to the bloodlines. "They made a crossbred dog," she says, "and it is mean."

The aggressive dogs seen today are a product of the new kind of owner, according to Nugent. "There are a percentage of them out there now that are people-aggressive," she says. "But it's not a large percentage compared to the overall population and we don't even consider these to be American pit bull terriers or American Staffordshire terriers."

This reputation for toughness and blood-lust gives them great appeal to the lowest segment of society. The dogs may be used for any number of criminal activities, from fighting, to guarding stolen property, drug labs or grow ops, to personal protection and intimidation. Because Schneider chose the presa Canario, a breed larger than most pit-bull-type dogs, he likely intended to make use of their fierce guarding abilities. "The people that have ego 'holes' look for the toughest dog and the meanest dog, and don't have a lot of control over the dog," says Kilcommons.

Today, dogfighting enthusiasts fall into one of three loosely defined categories: the professional-level dogfighters, the "hobbyists" with one or two dogs that only participate locally on a more casual basis, and the "street" fighters, who pit their dogs against each other in abandoned houses, alleys or empty yards. While professional fighters are willing to pay huge fees for carefully bred dogs, hobbyists and street fighters may get their dogs from all sorts of places: "free to good home" ads, backyard breeders, or shelters. Some are the cast-off survivors from professional fight rings.

Although dogfighting is illegal in all 50 states and throughout Canada, law enforcement officials and animal control workers still see evidence that this activity is alive and well in the dark underbelly of society. "It is a criminal code offense to be caught encouraging, aiding, or assisting in dogfighting," says British Columbia SPCA officer Liz Devos, "but people have to be caught in the actual act, which makes it difficult to get them. Sadly, there is no offense for someone who raises the dogs for fighting."

Even where it is an offense, prosecution is fraught with legal loopholes. In Oregon, the rules are possibly the toughest. Owning fighting dogs, participating in fights and watching fights are all felony offenses; even possessing dogfighting paraphernalia is illegal. But in Idaho, while *participating* in dogfighting and *attending* dogfights as a spectator are both misdemeanors, *possessing* dogs for the purpose of fighting is legal. In Georgia, dogfighting itself is a felony offense, but there are no laws against being a spectator, or owning fighting dogs. In Wyoming, all these offenses are considered misdemeanors only.

"Professional-level dogfighting is out of

control," says Mike Roach of the Anti-Cruelty Society in Chicago, Illinois. "It's bigger than big." It engenders the same level of hype associated with professional boxing, he states, except it's all underground. The Humane Society of the United States, which records dogfight reports, estimates that approximately 40,000 people earn their living solely from professional, organized dogfighting. These people will often travel from state to state for fights. They sell puppies across the country and even outside the country. According to the Humane Society of the United States, the minor penalties imposed for misdemeanor offenses are often considered by dogfight entrepreneurs as just another cost of doing business. The money generated by admission fees and gambling far outweighs the fines potentially incurred from breaking the law. The purse for one night of fighting could be as much as $50,000; some spectators will bet $10,000 on a single fight. Given the illegal status of the activity and the money involved, it's not surprising that dogfight operators and spectators are often involved in other crimes such as car theft, drug dealing, weapons smuggling, and money laundering.

Dogfighters invest a great deal of time and money in their dogs and are very proud of what they can do. "As word travels through the dogfighting world," says Roach, "their reputation starts to build." But the people and places involved are closely held secrets. Details are shared through coded messages and password-protected Internet websites. Fights between well-known dogs can draw crowds of spectators, some of whom will travel as far as necessary to attend. Because of the noise and cars associated with such crowds, Roach notes, more and more often professional fights are being held in rural areas. "You'll get anywhere from fifty to a hundred to two hundred people," says Roach. "There could be only two dogs, or there could be several. You're going to have weapons, drugs, alcohol, and big money."

Successful raids on suspected dogfight rings lead to houses and barns lined with cages. Inside lie clues: "break sticks," (stout clubs used to pry open the clamped jaws of a dog); blood-spattered walls; treadmills (used for endurance training); prong collars; heavy chains; padlocked collars. Because owners seldom seek veterinary care for their dogs, investigators often find a vast array of medical supplies, including such things as gauze and tape, suture material, staple guns, scalpels and surgical scissors, intravenous fluids, needles and syringes, as well as injectable vitamin K (to promote blood clotting), antibiotics, steroids, painkillers, and other drugs to which only licensed veterinarians have access. Sometimes the dogs themselves are found, chained to doghouses or lean-tos, at evenly spaced intervals in "yards." The American pit bull terrier is the fighter of choice, but large aggressive breeds like the presa Canario, the cane corso, the tosa inu, and the dogo Argentino are also popular with dogfighters.

Professional dogfighters groom their dogs for success even before birth. "It is the most brutal form of selective breeding," says Coren. "The dogs that win the most are most likely to be bred with other dogs that win the most. With these game-bred dogs, it's getting so bad that they have to take the litter away from the bitches at five weeks or she'll kill the pups. It's really quite scary. These particular dogs, the game-bred lines, have a very low threshold for violence." Many of these fighting breeds commonly have their ears cropped as puppies, a controversial cosmetic practice also performed on other breeds. But for fighting dogs it has a grim, practical purpose: to give their opponents as little as possible to grab onto.

Puppies are carefully observed for fight potential, and encouraged to play hard and rough. To build stamina, fight prospects are run on a treadmill or a "jenny"—a circular merry-go-round-like contraption. To help maintain interest, a cage with "bait" is placed in front of the dog, just out of reach. As the pups mature, 5 to 10 minute "rolls" or training fights are staged against other dogs, to give the pup experience with a variety of fighting tactics, without being seriously beaten up. After the bout, praise and rewards reinforce the lesson that his job is to fight on command.

Once a dog has successfully completed his training, the first match is scheduled. Several weeks of intensive training then ensue, complete with a strict diet and supplements, often including anabolic steroids. On the day of the fight, both dogs are weighed and must meet the previously agreed-upon weight. Water is usually withheld prior to a fight, in hopes that slight dehydration will decrease bleeding. The handlers switch dogs and each dog is washed down to ensure that no poisonous substance has been rubbed into their opponent's coat.

A fighting pit consists of a 16 feet x 20 feet (4.8 m x 5.5 m) boxed-in area. The floor is usually covered in carpet or some other material that won't become slippery when covered with blood and urine. At two opposite corners sit the "scratch lines," behind which the dogs are held prior to the fight. When the fight begins, the dogs attack each other until the judge sees one of them "turn," moving its head or shoulders away from the other dog. The dogs are then separated, taken to their respective corners, and sponged down. Then they are released again. The dog that "turned" must cross the scratch line, initiating the fight. A dog that refuses to scratch forfeits the match.

Street-level fighting, while not as organized, is every bit as vicious. According to Roach, dogfighting goes hand-in-hand with gang activity. A big, aggressive dog at one's side, especially one with a heavy chain collar, immediately creates a certain "don't mess with me" image, but for these individuals the dog's value is not as a companion, but rather as a legal and potentially lethal weapon.

"It's the gangbangers walking through the

neighborhood with their dogs that I worry about," says Roach, a former police officer. "They have an impact on the community, making people prisoners in their own neighborhood. People know they have to be in by three in the afternoon, because that's when the punks come out. People can't leave their dogs out in the yard because they'll be stolen and used for bait."

The hobbyists and gang-bangers who fight dogs use a variety of other "training" techniques, most of which are ineffective at best and inhumane at worst. "They believe starvation is a way of building up aggression," says Roach. "Keep 'em hungry, keep 'em lean, keep 'em mean." The dogs often live in filthy yards, staked to car bumpers, carrying 20 pounds (9 kg) or more of padlocked chain around their necks.

Chicago's Anti-Cruelty Society states that there are widespread community ramifications to dogfighting. According to a survey reported by the Society, Chicago's school children are almost universally aware of dogs fighting in their neighborhood. One out of every six children admits that they have attended a dogfight. Growing up surrounded by such activity desensitizes children to the suffering of animals and promotes violence as a normal part of life. The noises and odors arising from illegal kennels for breeding, training, and housing fighting dogs can even reduce property values. Observers may feel that the penalties for dogfighters are too insignificant to justify jeopardizing their own safety by reporting suspect neighbors.

Jeff Armstrong, who lives in a suburb of Chicago, became all-too-well acquainted with irresponsible owners and problem dogs when his son Ryan was severely mauled by a stray dog. "We know that the gangbangers, and whoever else is in this, are in it for the money. Go after them—they are the source! Doing so would have a huge impact on the dangerous dogs that are left for dead when they do not win fights any longer and then run after our children and family members," he says. "This is what must stop."

At the end of a fight, dogs are left with savage injuries: shredded ears, shattered jaws, crushed muzzles, broken limbs, punctured eyes. Even the dogs that "win" often die later, of blood loss, shock, or infection. "The owners are very proud," says Roach. "If the dog loses, their reputation is shot. The dog may die right there of wounds or trauma, or he might die because of the owner's embarrassment. [The owner's] macho image is shattered or tarnished, and he might just light that dog on fire or shoot it." The message is clear: *we don't tolerate losers.*

"When you mention dog attacks, no one wants to talk about 'dogs,'" says Karen Delise, author of *Fatal Dog Attacks.* "Everyone wants to talk about 'pit bulls.'" She began writing her book after a local incident in which a young child was attacked and killed by a dog. "You see all sorts of dogs barking or snarling, or chasing kids on their bikes, but the fact that one dog just took it to the ultimate degree kind of got me wondering. I began researching and collecting information about how frequently this happens but there were no circumstances attached to the information. As I became more interested, I saw that certain breeds were really taking a beating. Now, this did not start off as a breed issue for me. It was a general study into dogs, dog behavior, and the conditions in which these events occurred. I found it hard to believe that an ordinary dog, living in a house with ordinary people, could suddenly turn vicious.

"Breed is part of it. I'm not going to deny that certain breeds are involved in aggression more than others. But breed is not the biggest factor. We have this whole inner-city culture now, with substandard owners. No other breed has gone through what the pit bull is going through now, and their popularity is still as strong as ever. As long as they're still popular with bad owners, we're not going to get away from the problem."

When it comes to pit-bull-type dogs, statistics, like headlines, can be misleading. "Privately owned registries don't publish their numbers," comments Nugent, "so no one knows how many pit bulls are in the country."

"If you have 10,000 cocker spaniels and they kill one person," explains Delise, "that's one in 10,000. If you have 10 people killed by pit bulls but you don't know how many there are, you can't make a comparison."

Delise cites two reasons for this problem. First, only the UKC recognizes the APBT; the American Kennel Club does not. Second, most of these pit bulls are backyard-bred mixed-breed dogs. Don't know what to call it? Is it medium-sized? Does it have short hair? It must be a pit bull crossbreed.

"Pit bulls are considered such a huge liability a lot of shelters won't adopt them out," adds Delise. "With so many pit bulls being treated so poorly, the fact that they're *not* killing 200 people each year tells me there are a lot of good ones out there. It's important to get the information out that the American pit bull terrier is *not* the snarly breed people imagine it to be."

Good pit bull owners do everything they can to shed light on their dogs' good side. The American Temperament Test Society provides statistics on different breeds that have been evaluated. As of December 2004, 469 American pit bull terriers and 480 American Staffordshire terriers had been evaluated. Over 83 percent of them passed, just under the average 85 percent pass rate of the 680 mixed-breed dogs tested. This number, incidentally, is almost identical to the results for golden retriever, German shepherd, rottweiler, Saint Bernard, and Maltese breeds. The overall average pass mark for more than 25,000 dogs is 81 percent and Herkstroeter emphasizes that failures due to aggression are rare. Statistically, the APBT and the AmStaff have a higher pass rate than Chihuahuas, collies, dachshunds, Dalmatians, Cavalier King Charles spaniels, Yorkshire terriers, and toy poodles.

Bad Owner, Bad Dog

But obviously, people who breed and train their

pit-bull-type dogs for aggression are not going to have them temperament tested. It appears, therefore, that there are two tiers of pit bull fanciers. This is the crux of the problem. "A large number of these dogs have been specifically bred for fighting purposes," says Coren, emphasizing that these are "game-bred" dogs, American pit bull terrier and American Staffordshire terrier lines bred specifically for fighting. Certainly not all dogs of this type are bred for the pit. But how many generations away from such dogs are they? It can take years to breed out a negative quality. "Yes, there are lines that are bred reasonably well," he adds, "but anything with game blood in it is potentially a danger because of this specific breeding."

"You *can* breed dogs to a better temperament and that has, in fact, happened," he continues. When pit fighting was banned, English gentlemen demanded dogs that looked like fighters but had the temperament of companions. The English bulldog and the bull terrier were the result. "The bull terrier is *required* to have a 'sweet disposition,'" Coren says. "That's also what happened to the English bulldog. They look ferocious, but they're actually gentle companions."

Not so for the American pit bull terrier. "The UKC still has in its description of the APBT that it is dog-aggressive, not for inexperienced handlers," says Coren.

The worst dogs, he says, are usually bad because of a combination of breeding and environmental factors. "One individual I dealt with maintained that as far as he could tell, pit bulls may well be the most abused animals of all dog breeds," says Coren. "We saw the way these animals are being trained. They're half-starved chained with heavy chains. They run them on treadmills with a cat-cage in front of them. They reward the dog by letting him kill the cat and eat it. When one of those dogs makes it out into the street, you've got a surface-to-surface missile."

Besides the abusive training dogs receive in

these circumstances, there is the problem of questionable breeding practices. Careful screening of potential parents helps reduce the incidence of genetic health problems and most breeds have something to watch out for. Good German shepherd breeders test for hip dysplasia, for example. Cavalier King Charles spaniel breeders keep an eye out for heart problems. Responsible poodle breeders have their stock screened for eye disease. Doberman breeders improve their lines by neutering and spaying dogs that test positive for von Willebrand's disease, a blood disorder.

But in addition to physical soundness, ethical breeders look for psychological soundness. Dogs with any manifestation of temperamental instability, from excessive fear to aggression, would be culled from a breeding program. Breeders' reputations are built on the quality of the dogs they produce; every puppy that leaves their kennel is a walking advertisement of their knowledge of dog genetics. Good breeders work hard to make every puppy the best it can be. Responsible AmStaff and APBT breeders select for stable, non-aggressive temperaments.

But since irresponsible owners often seek out these dogs, breeders need to select for stable, non-aggressive *owners,* as well. If breeders sell dogs to individuals who go on to use the dogs for fighting or other illegal activities, Coren suggests that the blame be squarely divided between both owner and breeder. "The first line of culpability is with the breeder," he says. "Legislation should be done based on what the *dog* does, rather than what a *breed* does. Blame the breeder. Blame the owner."

But every breed of dog has its share of people who let their bitch mate with the neighboring dog because they both happen to be unaltered adults of the same breed. Trends and fads play a large role in this; poodles and cocker spaniels were nearly ruined 20 or so years ago because the demand for them led to a marked decrease in the quality of dogs produced. Now that "bully breeds" are popular, ignorant owners abound, happy to let their dog have a litter or two. While such a union may produce perfectly fine pet dogs, the chances are equally good that some of the puppies will have problems of some sort. Buying a puppy is always a gamble; the only thing prospective buyers can do is hedge their bets by doing their due diligence and looking for a responsible and meticulous breeder that cares about improving their chosen breed.

Ignorance is one thing. Far worse are those who deliberately set about breeding dogs specifically for aggression. For instance, dogs used for guarding the sites of criminal activities are obviously more effective when they are highly aggressive, highly dominant and poorly bonded with humans. Consider the names of some kennels boasting the production of "game-bred" dogs: Warlords. Devil's Den. Rockhard. Dirty White Boy. Mafioso. Most Wanted. Chaos. Stonekold. Schneider's kennel name was Dog O' War. Most claim that their dogs are not bred, raised or sold for illegal purposes. But when they also give their dogs names like Bone Crusher, Monster, Blue Gator, Dangerzone, and Dracula, one wonders what else we are to assume.

Hog-Dog Rodeos

Because of the clandestine nature of dogfights, enthusiasts don't advertise their dogs as "fighters." But there is another blood sport, one for which the penalties, if any, are even lighter. Hog-dog rodeos, often billed as "affordable family entertainment," feature trained attack dogs mauling wild pigs confined to a pen. Hog-dogs, also known as catch-dogs, are often game-bred pit-bull-type dogs, but other breeds are used as well: American bulldogs, Catahoula leopard dogs, Plott hounds, and Walker hounds. This activity likely stems from the legal use of dogs to hunt feral hogs, except that the dogs' primary task in that case is tracking and cornering the animal. In hog-dog rodeos, their only job is to attack. The pigs, whose sharp tusks are removed first with bolt-cutters, are still formidable foes;

both animals can be badly injured.

The HSUS believes hog-dog rodeos occur regularly in most southern states, including Mississippi, Texas, Oklahoma, and Georgia.
Whether used for pit fighting against other dogs
or against hogs, the same attention is paid to
producing aggressive game-bred dogs.

An Internet search for game-bred puppies revealed advertisements supposedly for
catch-dogs; the postings themselves, however,
are very revealing—both about the people who
trade in such dogs, and about what they do with
them. The following comments from breeders
are copied verbatim, spelling and grammatical
errors included:

```
"Gauranteed to catch or you get
another puppy, your money back,
and a bullet."
```

```
"You have to break her jaw loose
once she catches."
```

"... pit bull/american bulldog cross, great catch dog must sell, ate my dad's chickens."

"ONCE SHE CATCHES SHE IS LOCKED ON SHE HAS WON ALL 3 CATCH CON- TESTS THAT I HAVE BEEN TO AND I HAVE TO GET RID OF HER UNFORTU- NALLY IM ASKIN$100 BUT ILL TAKE A LAWN MOWER."

"... took him to the woods once an cought a 100 lbs sow with him that was when he was about a year old he has not been hunted since the i need to seel him i am about to go to collage and dont have time for him no more..."

Some of the advertisements were even more pointed.

"If you are looking to add some mouth and hard hitters to your yard then this little bundle of fire is the one for you."

"I only sell hard hitting awsome bullys."

"... have to get rid of her due to insurance reasons."

"Bitch is a nice catch dog, sire was a fighting pit."

"... lots of scars to prove her self."

"Will take down any dog quick."

"Bitch is the best catch dog on our place, and the father is an ex fighter."

And finally, the one that perpetuates every horrible stereotype of pit-bull-type dogs:

```
"IF YOUR LOOKING FOR A MONSTER
 LOOK NO FURTHER"
```

Genetics or Environment?

How much of this aggression is nature and how much is nurture isn't known, but we do know this: whenever a trait is selected for, it is more likely to occur. After birth, proper socialization (or lack thereof) will enhance the temperamental traits expressed by the puppies. The first two-to-three months of a puppy's life are crucial in forming its relationships with the world. A naturally fearful puppy that has many positive encounters with friendly people in different situations will gradually develop confidence about its ability to cope with a range of experiences. In contrast, the same puppy, if kept isolated, will be extremely threatened by strangers and unfamiliar situations. Nurture then, plays a large role in molding the inborn temperament of a puppy.

Nurture, however, can never cancel out the inborn temperament. "It's not black and white," says Coren. "I wish to hell it were. The genetic predisposition is there. Environmental factors can set off the genetically programmed aggression. Plus, there are also some breeds in which the results of a mistake are bigger. A rottweiler's jaw has 2,000 pounds per square inch of force. If he makes a mistake and bites someone, they're in trouble!"

Local SPCA officers recently brought a litter of three-to-four-week-old puppies to an animal hospital located near Vancouver, British Columbia, just minutes north of the United States /Canada border. The puppies, nine altogether, had been found in a box in a ditch, cold, wet, and starving. Three of them were dead. The remaining six were nursed back to health and fostered out until they were ready to be adopted. No one can say definitively what breed these puppies are, but they display the short brindle coat, the broad head, and the muscular bodies of pit-bull-type dogs. This scenario, unfortunately, is nothing new to shelter workers. Although many puppies of many different breeds are found abandoned each year, pit-bull-type breeds are definitely over represented. A higher proportion of irresponsible owners, unfortunately, are attracted to such dogs.

As these pups wrestled with each other, the largest male puppy displayed markedly aggressive play behavior. He clambered onto the neck of one sibling, latched onto the skin with his barely erupted milk teeth, and proceeded to grip and shake relentlessly while his littermate squealed. Bite inhibition, the ability to control the level of force inflicted, is learned during such puppyhood play sessions, and is usually taught by both the mother and the littermates. This puppy, however, had to be forcibly removed from his howling brother's back and segregated in his own cage. His mother wouldn't have tolerated such behavior from him, and would have let him know in no uncertain terms. None of his littermates will be strong enough to teach this brother to harness his biting.

Obviously, the playful but determined fighting exhibited by this puppy has not been taught or encouraged by humans with an agenda. It is simply part of his nature as a dominant male terrier, a trait that will have to be firmly squelched in his future home. Consider what would have happened to this puppy if he'd been allowed to grow up a few more months without proper boundaries.

When indiscriminately bred, poorly socialized dogs end up in shelters, they are evaluated as much as possible, but most of their history is a big question mark. They may appear to have inadequate early socialization and little or no training. Many shelters and rescues do temperament testing before adopting dogs out, but adoptive owners also need to understand that it's a gamble. The onus is on them to do their research and be prepared to invest time and money in the dog. Many, many shelter dogs become treasured family pets of impeccable character. But others come with baggage that they'll never be able to shed, even though it may be manageable with the help of a committed owner.

On the same day, in the same animal hospital, a vivid example occurred of what happens when the wrong person gets the wrong dog for the wrong reason. The SPCA had received a call late the previous night that a large dog was wandering alone in the downtown core of the city. When they arrived to pick him up, the shelter officer saw that the dog, a bull-mastiff-type breed, was weak with starvation and suffering from a nasty skin condition. When he was examined at the animal hospital the next day, the veterinarian who treated him found that the entire underside of his emaciated body, from his chin to his thighs, was swollen and hairless, covered in angry sores. Serum and pus oozed from the worst of his wounds. He guessed that this dog was probably only a couple of years old and had been confined to a small area to lie in his own excrement, for possibly his whole life. The smell was unbelievable. How he finally got free is a mystery, but one can speculate how the scenario began: someone got this dog with the intention of using him to guard their property. They put him in the backyard, or tied him to a stake, or a doghouse if he was lucky and, other than feeding him occasionally, forgot about him. Perhaps the owners got tired of him. Perhaps the dog barked and complaints were made and they decided to cut their losses. Perhaps a brave neighbor surreptitiously freed him. Perhaps the dog found a way out on his own. No one knows.

Antibiotics, medicated baths, exercise and proper food quickly put him on the road to recovery, but unfortunately, as soon as he started feeling better he became aggressive. Shelter staff had no choice but to euthanise him. What might have been a wonderful companion animal fell into the wrong hands and was turned into a sociopath.

CHAPTER 4

Risk Factors to Remember

All dogs have prodigious jaw power relative to their size. A single bite from a large dog is capable of causing tremendous damage to anyone on the receiving end. Such injuries often require extensive reconstructive surgery.

Dogs and Kids

There are two polarized schools of thought

about dogs and children. The first runs along the lines of "every child should have a dog," and is based on the assumption that kids and dogs are natural playmates. People who think this way often also consider dogs as protectors of children and expect that they'll watch over young humans with a kind of paternal or maternal care. On the other side of the issue are the people that eye all dogs as dirty, untrustworthy, potential child-killers. The truth, it seems, lies somewhere in between. "Dogs can be great for kids," says Kilcommons. "They teach children empathy and caring and intimacy in a safe format. But we need to identify dogs that aren't prepared for it or capable of it."

Because of their size, children—the most frequent victims—are usually bitten in the vulnerable throat, face, and head areas. In terms of fatalities, children under the age of one year are most likely to be killed by a dog attack. Within this category, the highest percentage of fatalities is among babies from birth to two months of age. After two months of age, the statistics show a sharp decline in fatalities. The fact that these are newborns and very young infants indicates that, clearly, the dog is initiating contact.

"Times have changed," says Kilcommons. "Today, many dogs function as emotional substitutes, many times emotional *hostages*. When young couples get a puppy instead of having a baby, they spoil the dog. They love it so much, but don't respect the dog enough to teach it. So no boundaries have been set and it turns into an obnoxious animal to have around." When such a couple decides to start a family, the situation changes and they may begin looking at the dog's behavior differently. "Everyone begins asking what they plan to do about the dog," he says. "They see it as a real threat to the baby, and many times, it is."

Unlike a dog biting the toddler who pulls on its ears, incidents with infants represent a different kind of behavior, one that appears to be a reaction to the presence of a creature that

US Fatalities Due to Dog-Bite Injuries Between 1965–2001 (Listed By Age)

Age of victim	Male victims	Female victims	Total
Under one year	38	41	79
1–4 years	112	52	164
5–9 years	61	21	82
10–14 years	12	1	13
15–19 years	0	2	2
20–29 years	2	2	4
30–39 years	1	4	5
40–49 years	4	5	9
50–59 years	6	4	10
60–69 years	5	7	12
70–79 years	6	15	21
80 years and older	7	15	22
Total	254	169	423

Source: Delise, Karen. *Fatal Dog Attacks*. Anubis Press, Manorville, NY, 2002.

is not only unrecognizable as a family member, but possibly unrecognizable even as human. A baby's sounds are strange, its smells are unfamiliar, and its movements are distinctly different from that of older humans.

Such injuries and fatalities may well be a result of curiosity, rather than aggression. "Many dogs don't know what to make of children," says Kilcommons. A dog can kill a child by attempting to pick it up as it would a puppy. Jumping into a crib can knock it over, crushing the child. There is not always malicious or predatory intent on the part of the dog.

"Since [babies are] relatively fragile, any bite is usually significant," explains Coren. But by two months of age, infants have changed dramatically. They smile. They've taken on the odors of the home and parents. Interactions have possibly taken place between the adults and the dog, about the child, that have helped the dog place the child as one of "the pack." It's at the bottom of the heap, a dog might reason, but the pack leaders mysteriously seem to value the strange creature, and therefore the dog must accept it.

The American Canine Foundation conducted a study into dog attacks between 1971 and 2001, during which there were more than 280 human fatalities. Of these deaths, 269 occurred in children under the age of eight, and in the vast majority, parental negligence was cited as a contributing factor. In several of the more horrific fatalities, the negligence defies belief: a days-old infant left alone on the floor of an unfurnished apartment with a malnourished German shepherd dog; a newborn baby abandoned in a garbage-strewn backyard with two pit-bull-type dogs. But there have been enough cases where the well-loved and cared-for dogs of responsible owners have displayed unexpected and inexplicable aggression towards newborns to indicate that wisdom errs on the side of caution. "When you have wee babes," says Coren, "you don't leave them unattended with a dog, even the most reliable dog you've got."

When toddlers and older children are bitten, the reasoning is a little clearer. "Most children, when they walk or run, appear to be quite uncoordinated," explains Coren. "To a dog, they appear to be like a wounded animal, and it triggers the predatory instinct. They also make high squeaky sounds. The combination is quite stimulating to a dog."

Kilcommons emphasizes that most dogs adjust beautifully to children. "We only hear about the ones that don't," he adds. "But common sense is at a premium. If five-year-old Jimmy is having a birthday party, put the dog in a crate. Not all children are taught how to be good around animals and it's way too much stress for the dog to be put in that situation."

Dogs and Chains

The junkyard dog guarding rusty car parts behind a high fence is a stereotypical villain, but while such dogs may or may not be dangerous, they are not statistically the biggest threat. They look dangerous, and therefore they're usually avoided. The familiar Labrador or Border collie tied up on the lawn across the street doesn't have the same image, yet the average child is more likely to be bitten by a dog they know than by a stray or strange dog. Three-quarters of all biting dogs are owned by the victim's family or a friend. Half of the attacks occur in the home or another familiar place. But a huge, and often surprising, predictor is the presence of a chain. Ten percent of fatal dog attacks studied by the American Canine Foundation involved restrained dogs on the owner's property.

Data indicates that chaining a dog is the most dangerous way to keep him. There are several reasons for this. A dog that is kept on a chain is likely not a "pet" in a true sense of the word. A dog kept primarily for companionship stays, for the most part, with the humans who keep it. If the people are in the house, the dog is in the house. If the people are outside, the dog is outside too. A dog routinely chained in the backyard is not exposed to the normal activity of home life and cannot possibly have the same relationship with its humans. Likewise, the humans who keep such a dog are also unable to have the same emotional bond with it as would those who live side-by-side with their dog. Keeping a dog restricted with a chain implies that the dog cannot be otherwise controlled. Nor is it supervised.

From the dog's point of view, living at the end of a chain is extremely stressful; such an environment provides insufficient social, mental, and physical stimulation. A dog under this kind of constant stress is at a higher risk of harmful behavior, even though he may appear calm. "In 1986," writes Karen Delise in *Fatal Dog Attacks,* "nine of the 15 fatalities by dog attacks were inflicted by chained dogs."

Even well-meaning people who approach a dog entangled in a chain are at high risk of being bitten. In this situation, the dog's confinement stress is immeasurably heightened; he may also be injured and in pain. Under such circumstances a dog has no ability to understand the good intentions of a would-be rescuer.

Dogs are animals built with the ability to travel great distances, to establish their home space and to protect that space. To restrict a dog's space to the limited circumference of a chain's-length can create in him huge defensive anxiety. Any encroachment on that space will be threatening to him, as there is so little of it. "It ain't much, but it's mine," might be his thought. Entering such a dog's zone can stimulate a wildly over-reactive territorial aggression and a threatened dog on a chain has no choice but to stand his ground and fight. A similar response is seen in some dogs when on a leash, particularly with other dogs. Dog-on-dog leash-aggression is a frustrating behavior exhibited by many dogs with otherwise fine self-control.

"We know how to make a dog vicious," says Coren. "You chain it on a very short chain. You allow only one person to interact with it. Then you have various people randomly come by and threaten it. Take any animal and put it on a tie-out like this and you could make it vicious."

The Family Dog?

In reports of dog attacks, many dogs are simply referred to as the "family dog." Mention is usually made of a prior uneventful relationship with the dog. But deeper investigation often reveals a far less integral role in the household. According to Kilcommons, the basis of all dog-training programs is establishing social structure for the dog, and insisting on the behavior appropriate to its place within that structure. "There's a tremendous amount of confusion in the public's way of thinking," says Kilcommons, who has websites called *www.familydoginc.com* and *www.mysmartpuppy.com*. "They're getting puppies and not raising them properly through proper socialization and early training. If you want to be successful with a dog, you're talking leadership and that means being clear, teaching what you want, and being consistent."

Just as there is rarely any distinction made between a dog that lives primarily in the backyard and a dog that lives in the house, the other important factor often overlooked is the length of time the dog has been in residence. There is a huge difference between a dog that has been in the family for a few days and a dog that's been with the family for a few years. Newly acquired dogs, particularly when obtained as adults, have clearly developed personalities and patterns of behavior. They've had many experiences and formed appropriate (to them!) responses to use in various situations. It was predictable that Bane, a mature, intact male, would be aggressive in his new home; not only was he untrained and insufficiently socialized, but also he'd only been with Knoller and Noel for about four months when he killed Diane Whipple. Until a dog has been with a family, in close association, under many different situations, for a substantial length of time, that dog cannot be considered, by any stretch of the imagination, to be part of the family.

In 1983, in Cincinnati, Ohio, an 11-year-old boy was killed by what was referred to as "the family dog." But the facts speak otherwise. The dog, an intact male pit-bull-type dog, had been purchased two weeks before the attack. The person selling the dog was later found to have stolen it and quickly sold it to prevent the theft from being discovered. The victim's family purchased the dog with the intent of using him to guard their home, as well as in hopes of breeding it to the female pit bull they already owned. The dog was chained at the time of the attack. Nearby, the female dog was also chained. No one knows the exact circumstances surrounding the attack, but at the end of it, the boy was dead. When the story made headlines, the original owner identified the dog as his, noting that the dog was in poor condition and had lost weight. Here is a situation with several large risk factors: a newly acquired dog, kept on a chain, near an intact female, with people he did not know. It was a tragedy waiting to happen.

The dogs that killed Cassidy Jeter were repeatedly referred to as "family dogs" by the press. But, says Karen Delise, "They were kept in the basement! Sorry, but these dogs don't meet my definition of a family dog."

Free-Roaming Dogs

In the study conducted by the American Canine Foundation, 20 percent of deaths involved unrestrained dogs off the owner's property. Whenever dogs are allowed to run together, the behavior of individuals within the group changes. Sometimes this change is subtle, sometimes it is dramatic. "It's pack mentality," says Kilcommons. "They're predators. You can have three nice dogs and one aggressive dog and they'll all follow the lead of the aggressor. The target can be livestock, other animals, or people."

All dogs find it exciting to be with others of their kind. This is evident even in the loosely controlled environment of an off-leash dog park. Immediately upon meeting, they will seek to determine where they fit into the hierarchy of the group. Much growling, raising of hackles and lips, and posturing usually takes place until everyone knows where they fit. There is heightened excitement and a potential for aggressive interactions, although for most well-socialized dogs with responsible owners, this potential won't be realized.

When dogs in a group are able to roam freely, unfettered by human interference, it's a different story. First of all, responsible owners do not allow their dogs to roam at large for hours or days on end, so it's safe to assume that such dogs have likely not experienced the bonding and training that a family pet would receive. These dogs are already at risk of negative interactions with humans. Put a number of them together and the potential for violence rises exponentially. Pack mentality is to dogs what mob mentality is to people.

Even single dogs that are normally confined can become unpredictable when faced

MINIMIZING THE RISK OF LOOSE DOGS

If a loose dog approaches outside, whether or not it appears dangerous, it can be very frightening to children. There are ways, however, to minimize the risk.

- Stand still. Dogs are naturally curious; standing motionless, with arms down, and eyes looking at the ground allows the dog to approach, sniff and hopefully lose interest. The average dog can easily outrun a person. Not only is running useless, it can stimulate the dog's instinct to chase.

- If the dog becomes threatening, teach your child to drop to the ground and curl up with fists over his ears, elbows tucked against his side. This position protects vulnerable neck and belly areas, and also puts the child closer to the ground. In pack mentality, the least dominant animals always take a lower, submissive posture in the presence of more powerful animals. Once submission is demonstrated, the dominant animal can leave.

with sudden freedom. According to news reports in April 2005, an 11-year-old boy was riding his bike in Kinnelon, New Jersey, accompanied by his Jack Russell terrier named Emily. A pit-bull-type dog living in an outdoor cage in a neighboring yard broke through the chain-link fence and attacked Emily. The little dog managed to get away and the boy was able to grab her and shelter her with his body. For several minutes, he protected her as the larger dog continued his attack. In the process, the boy suffered many bites and puncture wounds to his hands and face. A deliveryman happened on the scene and called 911. The boy was taken to a hospital, treated and released. Emily, however, was nearly killed in the attack.

It's a fact that attempting to protect a pet from an attack by a dangerous dog makes one susceptible to collateral damage. Such attacks are often not reported as "attacks on humans" as such; rather, they are viewed as injuries sustained due to interfering in a dogfight. Yet how could one stand idly by and watch a beloved companion be brutalized?

In his book, *Good Owners, Great Dogs,* Kilcommons describes how to help your dog with the least risk to yourself. "If a fight does erupt, do not try to grab your dog's collar," he writes. "This will get you bitten. Instead, grab a rear leg or the base of the tail, lifting up and back. This will stop the attack, yet keep you in a safe position."

Kim Moeller cautions dog owners, especially inexperienced dog owners, to learn what constitutes normal canine behavior. A great deal of dog play includes what *appears* to be aggression but *isn't*. It's important to know the difference. "Often, it's just a few scuffles and everyone gets upset," she says. "Dogs fight over resources or food. A lot of them are just under-socialized. Some of them are the rowdy types that are hyper-motivated to play and don't really have a lot of put-off signals. Mainly what we do is just normalizing dog play and dog behavior for people." A graduate of the Academy for Dog Trainers, run by Jean Donaldson, Moeller has been with the San Francisco SPCA for the past eight years and specializes in dog-to-dog aggression. "I do rehabilitation for shelter dogs, both on-leash and off-leash," she says. "If they are under-socialized or aggressive towards other dogs, I work on that with them while they're here. We see a lot of on-leash reactivity, barking at other dogs while on leash. I also teach a Growly Dogs class for dogs who bark on leash at other dogs."

When a dog is charged with the crime of biting another dog, it's important to quantify the injury. "If the dog made contact, did it break skin?" asks Moeller. "If it broke skin, was it more of a scratch or was it a puncture? If it was a puncture, how deep was it? We take punctures pretty seriously. I would take it seriously if I was taking on a case." A dog that makes contact, but causes no damage is showing excellent bite inhibition, what Moeller calls a "good mouth." But she reminds owners that they must take other factors into consideration, as well. "If it's an ear that's bitten," she says, "well, ears tear really easily. If it's the neck or throat or back, that's different." A dog that draws blood in a thick-skinned area, perhaps through a full hair-coat, that's a dog that means business.

Bite Prevention

There's no foolproof way to prevent dog-bite injuries. What we can do is use our knowledge of canine behavior to minimize the risks. "A lot could be accomplished by simply heeding a tired old dog-trainers joke," writes Janis Bradley in *Dogs Bite: But Balloons and Slippers are More Dangerous*. "Question: 'How do you approach a strange dog?' Answer: 'Never.'"

CHAPTER 5

Good Puppies, Safe Dogs

To live well with humans, every dog needs two things: socialization and training. Socialization is a matter of exposing dogs to many, many different experiences, places and people during puppyhood, to help them understand their place in the world. Basic obedience training takes this a step further, helping the dog understand his relationship to humans. When it comes to preventing aggressive behavior,

Kilcommons says there are specific techniques dog owners can use. "People are turning dog training into brain surgery," he says. "It's not." The first thing he suggests owners do is establish clearly that they are in charge. They demonstrate this visually by simple things like insisting that the dog walk on a loose lead, beside or slightly behind the owner, and that they always let humans precede them through doors.

Kilcommons also emphasizes that the issue of personal space is very important. Dogs must always defer to humans, no matter how inconvenient it might be. "As soon as the dog growls on the couch, it loses all furniture privileges," he says. "It might be his house, but who pays the mortgage?" The same rules of courtesy that work in the human world work against us with dogs. Kilcommons observes that many people constantly walk around their dogs, or step over them, instead of insisting that they get out of the way. This sends the wrong message to the dog. "I want the dog to give ground," he says.

"The thing with aggression isn't the action," he emphasizes. "It's the thought. People must recognize when the dog's thinking is off." He describes a typical scenario, in which a dog barks when someone is at the door. "Their job is to warn you," says Kilcommons. "You tell them 'good dog, you did your job and I am now taking control.'" He also advises owners to teach their dogs that when meeting people, the humans do the initiating, not the dog. "The dogs that come plowing into you, butting you, jumping on you, they're all over your personal space," he says. Instead, use the "sit" command to reinforce the hierarchy. "If the dog has to sit to be petted, or to go out, or to get a treat, it immediately puts the dog in the right social zone. The submissive dog stops at about the same distance we shake hands with."

Puppies need to learn early to accept human leadership, to allow humans to do simple things like clip its nails, look in its ears or mouth. Not only are these actions necessary to care for your dog, they remind the dog that humans are in charge and they can be trusted. But not all dogs submit willingly at first. "When a puppy starts to struggle, bite, scream or whine, I wait," says Kilcommons. "Okay. You can run through your hissy fit. As soon as you relax and are quiet, bingo." Only when the puppy has allowed him to do what he wants does he release it. With some puppies, these "handling lessons" need to be done in stages.

Puppies also need to learn appropriate behavior with other dogs. Moeller suggests reinforcing bite inhibition by removing a dog from play if he gets carried away. "He gets a time out," she says. "If he's rude again, it's another time out. A puppy that's not listening to the other puppy's signals needs to be reminded." She also suggests what she calls "social therapy," playtime with temperamentally stable adult dogs that won't hesitate to teach appropriate play skills.

Better Behavior Through Exhaustion
Because many of the working, guarding and

terrier breeds have tremendous energy, they usually need lots of regular, hard exercise; without sufficient exercise their behavior may deteriorate. Whether the dog becomes aggressive or simply obnoxious, poor behavior damages the human-animal bond. There are many socially acceptable and non-violent ways to exercise a dog, and allow him to use his innate abilities. If walking or jogging or playing ball in the backyard isn't enough, try out some specific dog sports.

- Weight-pulling competitions are a great opportunity for powerful dogs to show their stuff. Bully breed dogs excel at this sport, sometimes pulling weights of over 1,000 pounds (450 kg).
- Obedience trials demonstrate a dog's ability to obey commands with precision and accuracy. Successful teams demonstrate beautifully the appropriate relationship between dog and handler.
- Agility trials also highlight the bond between dog and handler, as well as the intelligence,

speed, and grace of the dog, by sending the dog over a course of jumps, walks, tunnels, and other obstacles.

- Flyball is a hugely popular relay race in which dogs leap over a series of obstacles, to a box containing a ball, then race back to let the next dog get started. It's a simple process but the dogs that love it, love it a lot!

From scent tracking, herding, and search-and-rescue, to pet visitation and pet therapy, there are many, many healthy activities to choose from.

But for some dogs, no matter how much exercise they get, they still want more; for these, inventive owners have come up with a variety of healthy activities the dog can do on its own. "Boomer balls" are large, hard plastic soccer-ball sized balls that many dogs enjoy chasing around a fenced yard. For dogs with boundless enthusiasm for tug-of-war, consider installing a spring-pole. Attach a piece of sturdy material such as burlap or rope to a spring or flexible inner tube.

Suspend it about five feet (1.5 m) above the ground and watch your dog fly! For dogs with strong bite drive, this is a great way to satisfy this need and give them a good, hard workout.

Although some of these tools are associated with fight training, that doesn't mean the tools themselves are suspect. "I don't have a problem with treadmills or spring-poles," says Kilcommons. "The dog needs the exercise and the outlet. This issue is control: Can you say 'out' and the dog will come off the spring-pole?"

Protection Sports

In the world of working dog sports are two activities that are particularly popular for dogs with strong bite drive: Schutzhund and Ring. Schutzhund is a German sport that evolved from activities used to test working dog abilities. It involves tracking, obedience, retrieval, some agility, and bite work: protecting the handler from a decoy assailant with a padded arm. The dogs must bite only on the padded area, must stop biting on command and must guard the assailant without further aggression. Ring sports of several varieties, including French Ring, Mondio Ring and Belgian Ring, are personal protection sports as well but they differ from Schutzhund in that there is no tracking and the decoys wear full body suits, allowing the dog to attack anywhere on the suit. Properly trained Schutzhund and Ring dogs are formidable allies, under immaculate control and willing to do anything necessary to protect their handler. However, like playing with fire, those involved in such sports understand that there are risks. New dogs, poorly trained dogs or unstable dogs will be unpredictable and harder to control.

"A lot of these are "hot dogs," aggression-prone dogs that are easily stimulated, and go to a high level of aggression quickly," says Kilcommons. "There are people in the sport that truly respect the sport and the dog. But others, their egos are in the front. They're not looking for a balanced dog; they're looking for an aggressive dog. You need to look at the individual."

Protecting dogs from abuse by criminals is only one small part of reducing the problem of dangerous dogs in the community. Far more visible, and likely to impact the average person, is the dog down the street. No matter what breed they own, all owners have a responsibility to train their dog to be upstanding canine citizens and good ambassadors for canines everywhere.

CHAPTER 6

Dangerous Dog Legislation

"In 2001, my now 12-year-old son Ryan was attacked and almost killed by a dog," says Jeff Armstrong. The boy was playing outside their home near Chicago's O'Hare International Airport when a stray rottweiler confronted him. When he reached out his hand, the dog attacked. Friends were able to drive the dog off, but not before Ryan had been severely mauled. Bite wounds to his chest nearly penetrated his lung, and one thumb had to be surgically reattached.

Armstrong was furious to learn that at least two prior complaints had been lodged against the dog. "When Ryan was lying in the hospital, I wanted every large breed of dog banned in this country," he remembers. But as his son healed, Armstrong cooled down and came to another conclusion: the owners are at fault, not the dogs. Surely, he felt, this owner would be held accountable for his animal's crime. Not so: he received a mere $200 fine and a six-month court supervision period. Astounded, Armstrong knew he had to take action. "At the time, Illinois had no laws on the books to handle crimes regarding dangerous dogs and irresponsible owners," he says.

He started making phone calls. "During the first phone call I made to my state representative pushing for this legislation, I mentioned I did not want the bill to go against any breed, and he agreed. I wanted to target the people responsible for these dangerous dogs, the irresponsible dog owner." But before he knew it, a breed ban proposal was underway. "The alderman claimed that pit bulls are responsible for the majority of dog attacks," says Armstrong. "Well, according to the information I obtained, which is public record from Chicago Animal Control Department, out of the 2,300 reported dog bites/attacks, 519 were believed to be by a pit bull. What about the other 1,781 dogs? Should we ban them also?"

Armstrong lobbied his state representative and the governor and eventually, his persistence paid off. "Governor Blagojevich signed the 'Ryan Armstrong Law,'" he says, "and now if your dog attacks, you can be charged with a Class 4 felony which can carry a five-year prison sentence and up to a $25,000 fine."

This, Armstrong emphasizes, is the way to deal with dangerous dogs. Banning specific breeds won't solve the problem. Only owner accountability will make the difference.

"I wanted to make sure that *all* dogs were included in Ryan's law, no matter how large or small," he says. "God knows I had a reason to ban all rottweilers. But controlling dangerous or vicious dogs is not about banning a breed; that's a quick fix. Then the next breed comes along and, oh, here we go again."

But, because certain breeds of dogs are over-represented in aggressive incidents, breed-bans are an ever-popular, knee-jerk response. According to *Fatal Dog Attacks* by Karen Delise, 36 breeds or types of dogs were involved in fatal attacks on humans in the United States between 1965 and 2001. But 85 percent of these fatal attacks were caused by 11 breeds or types of

FATAL ATTACK STATISTICS (BY BREED)	
Pit-bull-type	21%
Mixed breed	16%
Rottweiler	13%
German shepherd	9%
Wolf/dog cross	5%
Siberian huskie	5%
Malamute	4%
Great Dane	3%
St. Bernard	3%
Chow chow	3%
Doberman pinscher	3%
Other breeds	15%

Source: www.fataldogattacks. com/statistics.html

dogs, with pit-bull-type dogs accounting for 21 percent.

Given the weighting of attacks by pit-bull-type dogs, it's not surprising that all dogs of this type are eyed with suspicion. A single attack by a dog even resembling a certain breed is enough to create a reputation for viciousness in the entire breed. So why not simply outlaw such dogs? In the public hysteria that often follows dog attacks, this is the answer proffered by many municipalities.

Melanie Coronetz believes someone needs to be held accountable for the mauling deaths of her schipperkes. The dog that killed them won't be a repeat offender; he paid for his crime with a lethal injection. But the irresponsible owner who allowed him to run loose in the first place has never even been found, let alone punished, and since she wasn't bitten herself, no lawyers were interested in the case.

Despite her experience, she agrees with Armstrong that banning rottweilers is not the answer. She wants to see hefty fines and sentencing—perhaps with mandatory community service at an animal shelter—and even jail time, but she is against breed-specific legislation. She feels it's a *human* problem, not a *dog* problem.

No Bullies in Denver

Denver, Colorado, first banned pit-bull-type dogs in 1989, after a three-year-old boy was attacked and killed. Emotionally charged public meetings were held in city council to address the issue; tensions ran so high that some council members feared for their lives. The dogs were painted as vicious and bloodthirsty, with killer instinct always just beneath the surface.

Despite the reaction of some bully breed fans, who referred to the breed-specific ban with words like "holocaust," "Nazis," and "Ku Klux Klan," animal protection groups successfully fought the ban, and in the spring of 2004 legislation was passed forbidding Colorado cities from outlawing specific breeds of dogs. For one year, pit-bull-type dogs were legal in Denver.

It wouldn't last long. The city sued to over-
turn the decision and won. As of mid-April, 2005,
Denver reinstated the ban and pit-bull-type
dogs are no longer allowed within city limits.
Denver's ban, one of the toughest in the country,
makes it illegal to keep American pit bull terriers,
American Staffordshire terriers, Staffordshire
bull terriers, or any dog that resembles these
breeds. If found, they'll be confiscated, held for
one week, then euthanized. If claimed, a dog
is only released if the owner signs an affidavit
promising to remove the dog from the city. The
dogs are implanted with a microchip, making it
easy to identify them as having been previously
detained. Any such dog found within city limits
again will be immediately euthanized, with no
second chance. Between May and July 2005, police and animal control officials had impounded
nearly 400 dogs, most of which were destroyed.

Some owners of such dogs have chosen to
leave Denver. Others stay, but hide their dogs.
Others farm them out to friends or family living

elsewhere. But all are unhappy about it and disappointed that the long-time dispute couldn't be settled without resorting to such drastic measures.

The year 2005 was a difficult one for pit bull enthusiasts north of the border as well; within months of Denver's stringent ban, Ontario's attorney general, Michael Bryant, announced a province-wide ban of the dogs. It's not the first such ban in Canada; fifteen years earlier in Manitoba, following an attack that left a young girl badly disfigured, Winnipeg became the first Canadian city to ban the dogs. But a citywide ban is one thing; prohibiting pit-bull-type dogs across the entire province garnered much controversy. Unlike Denver though, Ontario instituted a grace period. Pit bulls owned by Ontario residents on August 29, 2005, or born in Ontario within 90 days of that date may be "grandfathered" in. They are allowed to remain, with the following provisos: the dogs must be spayed or neutered and they must be muzzled when out in public.

It's slightly more lenient, but still, owners of pit-bull-type dogs are furious. The majority of their dogs, they say, are loving and trustworthy. The few vicious pit-bull-type dogs that actually cause injury taint responsible owners of good pets. Such incidents make headlines, but they are the exception.

"There's a lot made of any dog-bite incident," says Sara Nugent. "Because of the history, people identify us whenever they hear 'pit bulls.' But most of the dogs that bite have no papers. They're mixes but they look enough like the APBTs or the AmStaffs that they get blamed. I used to think this has to be a coincidence, that I was becoming paranoid. But there are people out to get us!"

Experts Argue Against Breed-Specific Legislation

In 2000, the Centers for Disease Control and Prevention (CDC), the American Veterinary Medical Association (AVMA) and the Humane

Society of the United States (HSUS) joined forces to investigate whether or not breed-specific legislation works. Their findings, published in a number of scientific journals, indicate that banning breeds does *not* work.

"I have mixed feelings on breed-specific legislation," admits Stanley Coren. "I don't want the Staffie and the AmStaff to disappear. I think they've got a place; some of them have wonderful personalities. What you have to understand is that different breeds do, in fact, have different predispositions towards aggression. Within each breed there are also specific genetic lines of dogs. I would not recommend to any of my kids or grandkids to have one of them in the house, simply because I don't know if there's game breeding in the line. "But," he adds, "the flaw in breed-specific legislation logic is that if you ban one breed, something else will take its place."

"I've heard that the chow and the Akita are already being crossbred to replace the pit bull, if and when they get a ban in place," says Jeff Armstrong. "Here we go again. It will never end."

Enforcement is another enormous issue. Who decides what breed a dog is? On what criteria do they make this decision? As discussed earlier, there is significant confusion over the identities of the breeds involved, even among knowledgeable dog people. Since there's no such breed as a "pit bull," legal wording must specify which dogs it applies to. But, since the majority of the "bad" pit bull owners have unregistered, or mixed-breed dogs, the wording must be necessarily vague and inclusive.

A Labrador retriever crossed with a rottweiler would likely be similar in body type and head shape to a pit-bull-type dog. Does that mean such a dog should be impounded or euthanized? Uninitiated observers might confuse the small, short-faced Boston terrier or French bulldog with the smaller Staffordshire bull terrier. What about the many mastiff-type breeds, all physically imposing and powerful? Shelter workers may or may not have training in breed identification. Police officers and animal control officials may or may not have training in breed identification. Veterinarians may or may not have training in breed identification.

"Back in the mid-1990s, Berlin, Germany passed breed-specific legislation," says Coren. "There were about four or six breeds originally listed, with the caveat that any breed involved in biting could be included later on." Within four years, a whopping 40 breeds were listed. The Irish setter was even on the list of banned breeds, simply because of an incident in which a dog bit a child who poked him in the eye with a stick. Dog owners finally got together to protest the insanity. Before the 1999 municipal elections, crowds of dog lovers showed up to voice their disapproval. They were successful and the breed bans were discontinued.

Canada's National Companion Animal Coalition, comprised of experts from the Canadian Veterinary Medical Association, the Canadian

Federation of Humane Societies, the Canadian Kennel Club, and the Pet Industry Joint Advisory Council, was founded in 1996 to promote responsible pet ownership and enhance the health and well being of companion animals. The NCAC acknowledges that aggressive dogs present a real danger, but argues that breed-specific bans do not effectively protect the public from such dogs.

"What we desperately need, both in the United States and Canada, is some type of certification for the people that are being responsible," says Kilcommons. "The same irresponsible people that had these pit bulls are just going to graduate to a different breed that's also dangerous. They're just laying a foundation to outlaw dogs entirely."

Nugent agrees that there is a larger, darker force working against pet owners. "Humane societies have been infiltrated by animal rights people," she says, "and have sponsored breed-specific legislation in many areas." Animal rights proponents believe that all ownership of animals should be outlawed. They begin by advocating for breed-specific bans, citing the harsh treatment such animals often receive. "They say, 'We'll get rid of pit bulls for their own good because they're all abused,'" says Nugent. "Of course once they get rid of these, they move on to other breeds, then dogs in general. Their whole thing is 'let's prevent the breeding of all animals.'"

Nugent believes that breed-specific legislation is also being used to target other problems. Recently, she heard from a fellow AmStaff enthusiast who was panicking about a proposed pit bull ban in a Michigan county. Investigation revealed that the area in question was plagued, not with dog attacks, but with drug problems among children. The county hoped that, by legally entering to confiscate dogs, they'd be able to conduct drug searches at the same time. "They're going in through the back door," Nugent says. "They had had no dog bite cases to use as a reason." The ban was overturned.

Mike Roach also isn't in favor of banning specific breeds. But he argues that using animal laws as a "back door" is an effective approach to apprehending criminals, especially slippery drug offenders. "You've got all the information," he says, describing a typical scenario. "You get the warrant, you knock down the front door, but you find nothing; no drugs, no weapons, no money." Despite strong suspicion, there's nothing more they can do. The key to getting past this, says Roach, is for law enforcement officers to use the animal laws. "There's a dog chained up in the backyard," he points out. "That's the watchdog, they all have them. The dog has a heavy chain around its neck." The officers slap a misdemeanor on the owner for the chain, citing inhumane, cruel treatment, and impound the dog. "Before you can get out of the station, before the ink is dry on the forms, he's home, and he buys another dog," says Roach. Officers wait for the chain to appear, and then they go in again. "The second offense is a felony, and this time, you've got him," he says. "It's bye-bye for this guy now, and all by following the doggy laws."

Spay/Neuter Bylaws

The findings of the CDC, AVMA, and HSUS recommend that, instead of wholesale breed bans, municipalities adopt mandatory spay and neuter requirements. Because the vast majority of dogs involved in fatal attacks were intact males, pointing to the role of sex-linked aggression, this recommendation appears to have merit.

In February 2005, the California Senate proposed Bill SB861, authorizing local governments to enact breed-specific spay/neuter requirements, providing that no specific breed was declared potentially dangerous or vicious. Despite months of opposition from countless responsible California dog owners, the American Kennel Club, the Sacramento Council of Dog Clubs, and The Animal Council, on October 7, 2005, Governor Arnold Schwarzenegger signed the bill into law.

The following has been added to Part 6 of Division 105 of the Health and Safety Code:

CHAPTER 7.
SPAY/NEUTER AND BREEDING
PROGRAMS FOR ANIMALS

Section 122330. The Legislature finds and declares all of the following:
(a) Uncontrolled and irresponsible breeding of animals contributes to pet overpopulation, inhumane treatment of animals, mass euthanasia at local shelters, and escalating costs for animal care and control; this irresponsible breeding also contributes to the production of defective animals that present a public safety risk.
(b) Though no specific breed of dog is inherently dangerous or vicious, the growing pet overpopulation and lack of regulation of animal breeding practices necessitates a repeal of the ban on

breed-specific solutions and a more immediate alternative to existing laws.

(c) It is therefore the intent of the Legislature in enacting this chapter to permit cities and counties to take appropriate action aimed at eliminating uncontrolled and irresponsible breeding of animals.

Section 122331.

(a) Cities and counties may enact dog breed-specific ordinances pertaining only to mandatory spay or neuter programs and breeding requirements, provided that no specific dog breed, or mixed dog breed, shall be declared potentially dangerous or vicious under those ordinances.

(b) Jurisdictions that implement programs described in subdivision (a) shall measure the effect of those programs by compiling statistical information on *dog bites. The information shall, at a minimum, identify dog bites by severity, the breed of the dog involved, whether the dog was altered, and whether the breed of dog was subject to a program established pursuant to subdivision (a) These statistics shall be submitted quarterly to the State Public Health Veterinarian.*

It's not a breed ban, but it is a breed-specific spay/neuter requirement that allows municipalities to create their own lists of suspicious breeds. Many dog owners, especially those involved in the world of purebred dog shows, are furious, because only intact dogs may compete for conformation titles.

The American Kennel Club makes a case for economic backlash as a result of the bill, citing these dedicated dog fanciers who keep intact dogs solely for the purpose of participating in conformation dog shows. Nearly 1,400 AKCsanctioned events took place in California last year, attended by hundreds of thousands of dog enthusiasts. Approximately 185,000 dogs were entered in those competitions, most accompanied by extensive entourages of owners, handlers, and families. Mandatory spay/neuter ordinances for certain breeds would automatically disqualify those dogs from competition. Dog show attendance would drop, argues the AKC, as would the number of shows held annually throughout the state.

Recent studies show that one mid-sized dog show on average supports the local community with an influx of over $665,000 per day. Furthermore, dog show exhibitors tend to stay in the area before and after the dog show, spending an average of $320 daily. AKC estimates that passage of SB861 could therefore result in millions of dollars of lost revenue for the state.

Although only a handful of breeds are likely to be affected by Bill SB861, the AKC fears that any number of breeds could eventually become targets, ultimately devastating the entire pure-bred dog fancy.

The AKC also insists that, instead of punishing bad owners, such breed-specific laws target good owners of purebred dogs. Owners of listed breeds who intend to use their dogs for malicious purposes will simply switch to a different breed, resulting in an ever-growing list of regulated breeds. Mixed-breed dogs, right up there with pit bulls and rottweilers in terms of bites, would be unaffected under such laws.

Proponents claim that SB861 is necessary because "irresponsible breeding contributes to the production of defective animals that present a public safety risk" but the worst of these "breeders" don't have purebred dogs registered with the AKC or CKC. Because their dogs may not even be licensed with the city, the only way to ensure compliance by all dogs is door-to-door investigation. The very owners such bylaws intend to stop will continue unchecked.

When properly enforced, California's existing dangerous dog law forces all dog owners to be responsible regardless of the breed they own. Clear guidelines for identifying and managing dangerous dogs will promote responsible dog ownership and prevent tragedies from occurring. The AKC emphasizes that enforcing leash laws, having generic guidelines on dealing with vicious dogs, and increasing public education to promote responsible dog ownership are all better ways to protect communities from dangerous animals.

Stanley Coren encourages dog lovers to band together to lobby for more effective legislation. "If you can organize the dog owners, there's strength in numbers. One out of every four families lives with a dog. The big problem is they're unorganized. In the mid-90s in British Columbia, the Vancouver and Greater Vancouver Regional District began imposing draconian fines for off-leash dogs. But we had no off-leash areas." However, at municipal election time, dog-lovers got together and voted in dog-friendly people. This triggered an experiment that led to the many off-leash areas for dogs that Vancouver boasts today.

"Governments listen to the squeaky wheel," Coren emphasizes. "They hear about one dog that's terrorizing people and they don't hear about the 30,000 dogs providing comfort and succor. The one misbehaving dog of a particular breed gets all the press and we suddenly have breed-specific legislation."

Brian Kilcommons agrees that it's up to every dog lover to speak out. "If you have a dog running at large, especially a pack, or if there's someone in your neighborhood who's not responsible, take action. Notify animal control. Notify the bureaucracies. Send the message: 'You're responsible for these dogs' actions and you need to keep them contained.'" Individual actions can have significant results. If everyone on the street complains about a particular dog owner, that dog owner will eventually get the message. "Owners are going to start paying attention if they have to keep hauling their dog out of the pound."

During the months that Bane and Hera lived in Whipple's building, dozens of people had frightening encounters with them, and witnessed the inability of their owners to control them. "People knew about those dogs," adds Kilcommons, "but they didn't want to make waves."

Municipal bylaws have specific requirements regarding things like barking, identification, and licenses, and the use of leashes, but authorities seldom notice infractions unless individuals point them out. "Call your neighbors. Call animal control," says Kilcommons. Insist that such laws are enforced. "In Houston," says Nugent, "we had one judge who handled all the tickets handed out by the city animal control." The tickets carried a maximum fine of $200, but rarely, if ever, was this imposed. Most were thrown out, and the ones that *were* fined paid an average of $25. "These laws are not being en-

forced," agrees Kilcommons. "Instead, lawmak-
ers are laying additional laws on top of them."

Combating Criminal Dog Abuse

In the city of Chicago, dogfighting is considered
a premeditated, cruel, abhorrent practice that
deserves serious punishment. Dogfighting and
the possession of dogs for fighting are both felony offenses that can result in prison time and
fines of up to $50,000. According to the Chicago
Anti-Cruelty Society, recently convicted dogfighters in Chicago have criminal records that
include such significant crimes as assault/bat-
tery, arson, weapons charges, burglary, drug
charges, and attempted murder. Unfortunately,
attending a dogfight in Chicago as a spectator is
only a Class C misdemeanor.

Chicago has established a variety of av-
enues for combating animal cruelty and animal fighting. Chicago Animal Care and Control
(CACC) works closely with the Chicago Police
Department to help investigate allegations of

animal cruelty and animal fighting. Animal Control inspectors, officers, and veterinarians work together to investigate, arrest, and prosecute offenders. CACC supplies names, locations, and other information to law enforcement personnel and humane agencies throughout the area. They also provide shelter for animals confiscated during investigations.

Mike Roach believes this partnership between law enforcement and animal control is essential. To that end, he teaches animal cruelty law to police officers across Illinois and other states. "We teach them how to use the animal laws, and why to use them," he says. "If they get the call that there's a man with a gun or a rape in progress, they'll race to the scene with lights on and sirens blaring, knowing there's a chance they could be killed." But all too often, when police officers get a report of a dogfight in progress, the reaction is different, partly because the officers know there's little they can do when they get there. Investigating and prosecuting this activity is difficult, dangerous, and costly, unlikely to be undertaken without the prospect of felony charges. "There's a hole in the bucket," he says. "Strict animal code enforcement is the answer." When animal control officers or cruelty investigators work hand-in-hand with police, they are more likely to be successful in combating dogfighting as well as the crimes associated with it. "Police need to be educated," he emphasizes.

"We need to give police powers to all animal control officers, and/or cross-train the police departments to deal with these types of situations," agrees Jeff Armstrong. "Animal Control is limited in their authority. They cannot arrest anyone, they can only issue tickets."

The Humane Society of the United States offers a reward of up to $2,500 for information leading to the arrest and conviction of anyone organizing, participating in, promoting, or officiating at dogfights. Local humane societies and rescue agencies in many areas also have cash rewards for information leading to the arrest and conviction of dogfighters, as well as those involved in other forms of animal abuse. Individuals must pressure state legislators to change the laws to reflect the seriousness of this crime.

Canada's National Companion Animal Coalition (NCAC) has a variety of recommendations regarding dangerous or vicious dogs, and one of them is providing breed-appropriate physical exercise and mental stimulation. All owners who decide to share their lives with a breed of dog that has a reputation for aggression need to accept that, while this characteristic might never be expressed in their particular dog, the potential is always there. It is their responsibility to channel it into acceptable activities. To insist that their dog is harmless, especially if the dog has already chased other dogs, frightened people, or even bitten, is to allow a predictable situation to escalate, resulting, almost always, in the death of their dog.

NCAC has clear recommendations for municipalities regarding dangerous dogs:

- Owners should be fined heavily if their dog is involved in a bite incident.
- Instead of banning specific breeds, professional temperament assessment should be done on individual dogs considered potentially dangerous.
- Once dogs are professionally assessed as a danger to the public, a clear protocol should be in place, such as confinement or euthanasia
- Incentives should be in place for owners to spay and neuter, socialize, and train their animals.
- Leash laws, running-at-large laws, property confinement laws, and laws describing the use of muzzles should be instituted.
- Public education promoting responsible pet ownership should be implemented.

The focus of municipal intervention should be to prevent incidents from occurring. Banning an entire breed is ineffective for this purpose, in that some eliminated dogs are not dangerous, while some dogs excluded from the ban will be. Instead, it is more effective to determine what, exactly, constitutes a "dangerous" dog, and act accordingly. The NCAC suggests that a "dangerous dog" is:

- Any dog that shows threatening or aggressive behavior
- Any dog that is trained to attack
- Any dog that has killed, whether it be a person or a domestic animal, regardless of the circumstances
- Any dog that has bitten or injured a person or domestic animal. In this case, mitigating circumstances should be considered; a dog reacting to teasing, trespassing or defending its owner is acting in a reasonable manner.

Spaying and neutering of such dogs will reduce sex-linked aggression, as well as prevent them from passing on such tendencies to future generations of dogs. Municipalities might implement dangerous dog license fees, significantly higher than ordinary dog licenses. They could require that such dogs be muzzled and leashed when off the owner's property and strictly confined when on the owner's property, within a fence that the dog is unable to escape from, and that the public is unable to get into. They could ban chains or tie-outs. They could insist that warning signs be posted on yards containing a dog deemed to be at risk of aggression. They could impose heavy fines for non-compliance, increasing them for repeat offenses. The NCAC also suggests that, based on the severity and frequency of infractions, owners be forced to relinquish or euthanise such a dog.

"The penalties in Canada for owning a dog that bites vary from city to city," says Liz Devos of the BC SPCA. "Each city has its own bylaws which relate to dangerous dogs. I do know that if you own an animal that bites and have had previous complaints and the dog bites again causing injury or death, you can—and likely will—be charged with criminal negligence causing bodily harm."

Owners of dogs that injure other pets may or may not be held responsible. "The New York city council is working on a pet protection law which would make owners of dogs that maim or kill other pets criminally liable for such attacks," Coronetz says, "but the measure hasn't yet passed."

The pendulum continues to swing, pushed by public outrage and ignorance. "We live right now in a society where people just want quick answers to complex problems. They don't want complex answers to complex problems," says Karen Delise. "Nothing is black and white with living beings."

Amazing Facts and Figures

- The oldest known breed of dog is the saluki, which is an Arabic word meaning "noble one." Ancient Egyptians raised these dogs as hunting dogs. The oldest breed of dog native to North America is the Chihuahua.

- It isn't exactly true that one year in a dog's life is the equivalent of seven years in a human's life. A more accurate calculation is as follows:
  - At one dog year, a dog is the equivalent of 16 human years
  - At two dog years, a dog is the equivalent of 24 human years
  - At three dog years, a dog's age equates 30 human years
  - For every dog year after that, add four human years.

- A dog's mouth contains 42 teeth.

- The Doberman breed was created in the 1860s by Louis Doberman, a German tax collector, who created the dog to protect him while he worked.

- The problem of dog bites appears to be growing in the U.S. In a seven-year period during the 1990s, the number of dogs rose by two percent while the number of bites increased by 33 percent. The property/casualty insurance industry paid $250 million for dog-bite claims in 1995, $310 million in 2001, and $345.5 million in 2002. Additional losses were paid by other segments of the insurance industry, such as health insurers.

American statistics

- Almost 800,000 bites per year—one in six—are serious enough to require medical attention.
- Dog bites send nearly 368,000 victims to hospital emergency departments per year (914 per day). Getting bitten by a dog is the second most frequent cause of visits to emergency rooms.
- Every year 2,851 letter carriers are bitten.
- In the US from 1979 to 1996, 304 people died from dog attacks, including 30 in California. The average number of deaths per year was 17.
- The majority of dog attacks in the US (61 percent) happen at home or in a familiar place.
- An American has a 1-in-50 chance of being bitten by a dog each year.

Canadian statistics

- Injuries associated with dog bites and dog attacks were sustained most frequently by five to nine year olds (28.5 percent).
- Of all injuries related to dog bites and dog attacks, 57.9 percent were to males.
- Injuries occurred most often in the summer, 37.7 percent, and most frequently between the hours of 4 and 8 p.m. (32.7 percent).
- Most injuries occurred at the victim's own home, 34.2 percent, or at another home, 30.3 percent.
- The majority of injuries occurred when the patient had no direct interaction with the dog, 28.9 percent.
- Injuries that required advice only, or minor treatment, accounted for 57.9 percent of patients, while 36.8 percent of patients needed medical follow-up after leaving the emergency department and 4.5 percent were admitted to a hospital.
- Overall, the most frequent types of injury were bites, 73.1 percent, and the body part most often affected was the face, 40.5 percent.

Fatal Dog Attacks in Canada: 1983–2003

Year	Dog breed	Incident	Location
1983	Farm Dogs	Roaming dogs kill child	Edmonton
1987	German shepherd cross	Chained dog attacked child	Vernon
1988	German shepherd	Unsupervised child	Quebec
1990	Chow Chow	Attack on newborn	Ontario
1993	Sled dogs	Chained dogs kill child	N.W.T.
1993	Sled dogs	Attacked by loose dogs	Alberta
1994	Maremma sheepdog	Family dog killed child	Ontario
1995	AmStaffs	Drunken man provoked dogs	Ontario
1995	German shepherds	Killed by uncle's dogs	Saskatchewan
1996	Strays	Child killed by stray dogs	Manitoba
1997	Sled dog	Chained dog with pups	Saskatchewan
1998	Sled dogs	Pack chained on sea ice	Iqaluit

Year	Dog breed	Incident	Location
1998	Bull-mastiff	Playing with neighbor's dog	Ontario
1998	Lab/Husky crosses	Mother & son killed by pack	Newfoundland
1998	Strays	Boy killed by strays	Manitoba
1999	Husky cross	Neighbor's dog	British Columbia
1999	Husky	One of 24 chained dogs	Quebec
1999	Husky cross	Grandfather's dog	N.W.T.
1999	Strays	Girl killed by starving dogs	Alberta
2002	Labrador cross and rottweiler	Attacked in field	Ontario
2003	Rottweilers	Boy wandered into yard	New Brunswick
2003	German shepherd crosses	Grandmother's dogs	Manitoba

NATIONAL CANINE RESEARCH FOUNDATION figures. (While there may be some incidents missing from this list, it appears to be the only record of fatalities available for Canada, and may be considered a fair representation of the types of fatal dog attacks that have occurred in Canada over the last two decades.) Source: ncrf2004.tripod.com/id10.html

DOG SENSE

Most grade-school children know what to do if their clothing catches fire: stop, drop and roll. Firefighters teach it and children remember. But do they know how to safely pet a dog, or what to do if approached by a strange dog outside? Teaching them acceptable behavior can help reduce their risk of being bitten.

- **Always ask permission:** Never approach an unknown dog without asking the owner first if it's okay to do so. Once permission has been granted, extend the back of the hand, palm down, for the dog to sniff. Dogs learn a tremendous amount of information from their noses; giving them a chance to do this reassures them that you mean no harm. Then, stroke along the side of the back, moving in the direction of the fur.

- **Avoid sensitive areas:** Children tend to be impulsive, rushing in for a hug, stepping on a paw or pulling on a tail or ear. While many dogs will tolerate this, some are touchy, so children should be taught not to touch the face, feet or ears. After one serious mauling of a young child by a golden retriever, the distraught owners, who'd immediately had the beloved pet euthanized, requested a post-mortem examination. The necropsy revealed a severe ear infection, which would have made the affected area terribly painful to touch. Even gentle tugging on the ear by the child would have been excruciating to

DOG SENSE (CONTINUED)

the dog and explained how a previously gentle and trustworthy dog could have lost control so badly. It's a tragedy all around; if the ear infection had been discovered earlier it could have been treated. But if the child had known not to touch the ear, the incident might not have occurred.

- **Respect and obey the "no touch" times, when a dog is better left alone.** Like humans, dogs value their sleep and their food. The old adage about letting sleeping dogs lie has wisdom here. Likewise, don't try to pet a dog when it's eating or playing with or chewing on a toy. A dog that shows signs of disinterest, such as moving its head away, or standing stiffly during stroking, is probably just being polite.
- **Heed the warnings!** Dogs are gregarious creatures; they will initiate contact with people. If they avoid contact, there is a reason for it. Pursuing such a dog is asking for trouble. Frightened dogs often assume a lowered body position and attempt to move away. They may bark, they will often carry their tails low, tucked between their legs, and their ears may be folded back. "This dog is uncomfortable!" cautions Moeller. Teach your children that such dogs are armed and dangerous. Aggression that stems from other causes may look quite different. Happy dogs, according to Moeller, have open, relaxed faces, probably with their tongues out. This changes when

DOG SENSE (CONTINUED)

a dog is nearing the limit of his aggression threshold. "The eyes get squinty, the mouth closes," she adds. "He might start to curl his lip or show some teeth. This is a less tolerant dog."

• Never, never approach a tied or chained dog, nor one confined within a fence or pen. A dog at risk of aggressive behavior often tries to look as tall as possible, with his head and tail held upright. The fur along the back of his neck might be standing up. He will likely make direct eye contact—the classic sign of a dominant dog—and he will probably bark, snarl or make a show of "air-snapping." The tail might be wagging slowly but don't be deceived; this is not a dog that wants a friendly game. "We call this a 'flag tail'," says Moeller. Guard dogs, or household pets that feel responsible for protecting their people will display this behavior when their territory is threatened. Do NOT go near dogs displaying these signs!

Find the Pit Bull

For many people, a pit bull is a big-headed dog, or a dog with cropped ears. For some it's a brindle dog, or one with a patch on eye, or a big stocky dog. Breed misidentification is a dangerous thing during a time when breed-specific legislation is the proffered solution. Pit bull dogs are often blamed for dog attacks that may have been caused by another breed.

Only one of the photographs featured on the web site listed below is the real American pit bull terrier. Take the test to see if you can find it:

www.pitbullsontheweb.com/petbull/findpit.html

What Others Say

"The dogs have just become whipping boys for a lot of social issues."

Sara Nugent, President,
Staffordshire Terrier Club of America

"Most dogs think their names are "NO!" It's what they hear most often."

Brian Kilcommons, Dog trainer and
author of "Good Owners, Great Dogs"

"Understanding brain growth should dispel the nature/nurture controversy once and for all. It is never, ever either nature or nurture, but always both at the same time."

Raymond and Lorna Coppinger
Authors, "Dogs, A New Understanding of
Canine Origin, Behavior and Evolution"

"A lot of people compare some dogs to guns. They're not guns. They're thinking and making their own decisions."

Karen Delise, author of
"Fatal Dog Attacks"

"Dog bites are among the rarest of fatal mishaps. For every person who dies as a result of dog bites, lightning kills five. For every dog bite fatality, four people are killed by forklifts, even though a very small number of people actually come into contact with these machines."

Janis Bradley
Author of "Dogs Bite: But Balloons
and Slippers are More Dangerous"

"A dog that behaves in a predatory fashion toward other dogs will behave in a like fashion toward humans, to the extent he views humans as his social equals. And this may indeed explain the efficient and otherwise inexplicable savagery of attacks on humans by pit bulls and other traditional fighting breeds."

Stephen Budiansky
Author of "The Truth About Dogs"

"Aggression is not a pin-point thing; it's a general kind of thing. That's the real problem with these dogs. Genetics is not creating a trait. It's lowering the threshold, creating the likelihood that a behavior will be expressed in certain circumstances."

Stanley Coren, Ph.D.
Professor of Psychology,
University of British Columbia, Canada

"Pit bull owners probably know more about dog law than do any other kind of dog owners. They have to. Too often, pit bull owners have been the victims of breed-specific legislation that targets their dogs, attempting either to place restrictions on them or to ban them altogether. However, a five-year study (published in the Cincinnati Law Review) concludes that statistics do not support the assertion that any one breed is dangerous. Fighting breed-specific legislation, however, doesn't mean burying your head in the sand and denying that pit bulls (and other dogs) can seriously injure—and even kill—people."

Caroline Coile
Author of "Pit bulls for Dummies"

"I've always argued that people need to be held responsible for their animals. Hey, if you want to drive a Lamborghini, you're responsible. If you can't handle the car, and hit a pedestrian, you are held responsible. I'm not sure a presa Canario equates with an expensive sports car, but this is a breed that absolutely requires special handling. If you're reckless with a dog like this, then you should pay a price."

Steve Dale, journalist, host of Pet Central, and syndicated columnist of "Steve Dale's Pet World"

Interesting Web Sites

Stay Bite Free, a program from the Humane Society of the United States: *www.nodogbites.org*

The National Association for Humane and Environmental Education: *www.nahee.org/bite.asp*

Dog Scouts of America: *www.dogscouts.com/biteprevention.shtml*

Doggone Crazy, a board-game to teach children dog safety: *www.doggonecrazy.ca*

Dogs, Cats and Kids, a video by Dr. Wayne Hunthausen, available from: *www.catdoctorstore.com/p-dogs_cats_kids_video.html*

A disturbing and graphic illustration of the abuse many pit-bull-type dogs endure: *www.pitbullproblem.tk*

Bibliography

Bradley, Janis. *Dogs Bite: But Balloons and Slippers Are More Dangerous.* Berkeley, CA: James and Kenneth Publishers, 2005.

Budiansky, Stephen. *The Truth About Dogs.* New York, NY: Viking, 2000

Cleveland, Sierra and Campbell, Butch. "Out of the Pit, Dogfighting in Chicago", a documentary film. Izzy Works Productions, USA, 2003. www.izzyworksfilms.com

Coren, Stanley. *The Intelligence of Dogs.* London, England: Headline Book Publishing, 1994.

Coren, Stanley. *The Pawprints of History.* New York, NY: Free Press, 2002.

Coppinger, Lorna and Coppinger, Raymond. *Dogs: A New Understanding of Canine Origin, Behavior and Evolution.* Chicago, IL: University of Chicago Press, 2001.

Delise, Karen. *Fatal Dog Attacks.* Manorville, NY: Anubis Press, 2002.

Jones, Aphrodite. *Red Zone: The Behind-the-Scenes Story of the San Francisco Dog Mauling.* New York, NY: Avon Books, 2003.

Kilcommons, Brian and Wilson, Sarah. *Good Owners, Great Dogs.* New York, NY: Warner Books, 1992, 1999.

Kilcommons, Brian and Wilson, Sarah. *Childproofing Your Dog.* New York, NY: Warner Books, 1994.

Scott, John Paul and John L. Fuller. *Genetics and the Social Behavior of the Dog: The Classic Study.* Chicago, IL: The University of Chicago Press, 1965.

Popular Dog Series, Vol. 21, "Bully Breeds." Irvine, CA: Fancy Publications, 2002.

Popular Dog Series, Topic Vol. 9, "Training Secrets for Bully Breeds." Mission Viejo, CA: BowTie Inc., 2004.

Website References
American Veterinary Medical Association: *www.avma.org/pubhlth/dogbite/*

Centers for Disease Control: *www.cdc.gov/ncipc/duip/biteprevention.htm*

Canadian Hospital Injury Reporting and Prevention Program: *www.phac-aspc.gc.ca/injury-bles/chirpp/injrep-rapbles/dogbit_e.html*

Photo Credits